Railroad Convention

Northern Pacific Railroad

Proceedings of a convention held at East Saginaw, Michigan

Railroad Convention

Northern Pacific Railroad
Proceedings of a convention held at East Saginaw, Michigan

ISBN/EAN: 9783337141936

Printed in Europe, USA, Canada, Australia, Japan

Cover: Foto ©Andreas Hilbeck / pixelio.de

More available books at **www.hansebooks.com**

NORTHERN

PACIFIC RAILROAD.

PROCEEDINGS

OF A

CONVENTION

HELD AT

EAST SAGINAW, MICHIGAN,

ON THE

23d and 24th November, 1869.

TO CONSIDER THE QUESTION OF

THE SHORTEST AND MOST FEASIBLE ROUTE, AND THE
BEST MEANS FOR PROMOTING THE CONSTRUCTION
OF THE NORTHERN PACIFIC RAILROAD.

EAST SAGINAW:
Daily Enterprise Office

1869.

A Call for a Northern Pacific and Mich'gan Short Line Rail Road Convention, at East Saginaw, Michigan, November 23d, 1869.

The undersigned committee, appointed by the Common Council of East Saginaw to issue the call and make arrangements for a convention to be held in this city on the 23d day of November, 1869, at 2 o'clock P. M., respectfully and urgently request all municipal and other corporate bodies on the contemplated line of the Northern Pacific Rail-road, from the head of Lake Superior, *via* the Straits of Mackinaw, to the Atlantic, to send delegates to said convention.

And it is earnestly hoped that Boards of Trade, City Councils, county and township authorities, railroad corporations, and other bodies throughout the State of Michigan, will be fully represented; and that the States of Iowa, Minnesota, Wisconsin, New Jersey, New York, Connecticut, Rhode Island, Massachusetts, Maine, New Hampshire, Vermont, and the Province of Canada, will send delegates, especially from the Western States named, and from along the line of the route recently adopted by the Trans-Continental Railroad Convention at Oswego.

The following are among the important questions to be submitted for the consideration of the convention:

1st. Is there any necessity for more railroads across the continent? If so, what routes should be adopted?

2d. Is there any advantage to be secured to the Northern Pacific road by reason of its reaching water communication sixteen hundred miles from the Atlantic, at the head of Lake Superior?

3d. Comparative cost of transportation by rail and by water; time being considered money.

4th. Puget Sound as a western and Portland as an eastern terminus of the Northern Pacific Railroad.

5th. The route by the Straits of Mackinaw; is it the shortest and most practicable? Will it open and develop a region of country rich in soil, timber and minerals, and by reason of which, will it secure a vast amount of local traffic?

6th. Do the Central and Union Pacific Railroads supply such advantages to the country as to render it inexpedient for the Government to encourage the building of a Northern and Southern Pacific Railroad?

7th. Should the Government, in the present state of its finances, make further grants to railroads?

8th. The character of the country on the line of the Northern Pacific.

9th   The valleys of the Upper Mississippi and the Red River of the North.

10th.   The western slope of the Rocky Mountains to the harbor of Puget Sound.

11th.   The shortest line between China and Europe.

12th.   The railroads of the United States; do they tend to settle, develop and enrich the country ?

13th.   Would the granting of subsidies to two more Pacific railroads retar l or expedite the liquidation of the national debt ?

14th.   The railroads of Michigan as the shortest connecting links between the Northern Pacific Railroads and the roads from the East and South

15th.   The duty of the Government in reference to the future disposition of the public domain.

16th.   The present and prospective value of the agricultural, mineral, saline and lumber products of Northern Michigan

17th.   The future of the Northwest.

It may be observed that the title given to this convention, at the head of this call, implies that its object is local and not national in character.   To this we may reply that the Northern Pacific Railroad, thought to be a great national trans-continental line, is nevertheless local, so far as its route and *termini* are concerned, and it has been observed that the Trans-Continental Railroad Convention, recently held at Oswego, N. Y., was called with the express object of building an air line from Portland, *via* Oswego, Lewiston and the Detroit or St. Clair rivers, to Chicago, there to meet the Union and Northern Pacific Railroads; and, though that convention approved of the line to Chicago, it also approved of continuing the Northern Pacific from the head of Lake Superior, east, *via* the Straits of Mackinaw and the Detroit or St. Clair rivers.

This convention, then, cannot be considered any more local than the one at Oswego; though its chief objects shall be the building of the Northern Pacific Railroad through Michigan, across the Straits, to connect in the Lower Peninsula with all roads running east and south.

We are free to admit that, in view of her seven hundred miles of undeveloped territory, over which such a route would pass, the richness of her soil, the amount of valuable timber, her sixty thousand inhabitants in the Upper Peninsula engaged in developing her vast deposits of copper and iron, and who have no outlet except by water, and on account of her saline and other comparatively undeveloped elements of wealth, Michigan, perhaps, has a more vital interest in the object of the convention than any other single State.

But while this may be true, it is equally true that all the States named in the call are more interested in this than in any other route. This is made evident by a glance at the map, where it will be seen that this line will open up the northern part of Wisconsin, and afford a competing railroad outlet east, other than by Chicago, for wheat and other products of Iowa and Minnesota.

It will also appear evident that, should the Northern Pacific Railroad adopt no other line to the east than around the south end of Lake Michigan, (which is on the line of the Union Pacific,) its traffic would naturally drift to the South, and New York and all the New England States would be injured, and New Jersey to some extent, thereby.   It is not the object of the convention to oppose connections between the Northern Pacific Railroad and Chicago, but to secure a route also by the Straits, and thus to guarantee to the Northern and Eastern States what the Government intended by its grant of land—a Northern Pacific Railroad, to run as far as possible through the undeveloped portions of the States and Territories.

By this route, and the connections with Chicago, all railroads running south and east, and all the States on the Atlantic, would receive their just share and interest in a trans-continental raiload built by the liberality of their Government and the energy of its citizens.

To secure these objects, and to discuss the subjects embraced in this circular, the convention is called, and we again earnestly invite the presence of delegates and of all interested citizens from every quarter.

The undersigned also respectfully request all newspapers friendly to the objects of this convention to publish the call for the same. It was the intention to have the call signed by many leading citizens in this and other localities who approve of the convention, but the shortness of time, and the necessity for an early and extended notice, induces the committee to publish the call with their names alone attached.

And acting as we do, in harmony and in accordance with the desire of all favorably interested, we trust that the importance of the convention will not be diminished, or an interest in the same weakened, on account of the call not being more numerously signed.

Hoping that the response of delegates may be equal to the importance of the subject, we are, with high consideration,

JAMES L. KETCHAM, Mayor of East Saginaw,

C. K. ROBINSON, WM. J. BARTOW,

JOS. A. HOLLON, JEREMIAH FISHER,

GEO. W. PECK, JOHN F. DRIGGS.

GEORGE W. PECK, Secretary.

PROCEEDINGS OF THE CONVENTION.

FIRST DAY.

Pursuant to the preceding call, a Convention of Delegates assembled at Irving Hall, in the City of East Saginaw, at 2 o'clock, P. M., on Tuesday, November 23d, 1869.

The rear of the platform of the hall was covered by an immense map, exhibiting on a large scale the route, etc., etc. It was prepared by Messrs. Goddard, Kirby, Herbert and Eastman, and proved of great value in the deliberations, etc.

The Convention was called to order by Hon. Geo. W. Peck, and organized by appointing Hon. John F. Driggs of East Saginaw, temporary President, and F. H. Rankin, of Flint, temporary Secretary.

Mr. Driggs, on assuming the chair, addressed the Convention as follows:

GENTLEMEN OF THE CONVENTION :

I only express the sentiments of all the citizens of this valley, when I extend to you a cordial and kind welcome to this locality, and I know I express the regrets of our whole community that an unforeseen and severe storm has probably prevented the attendance of many delegates from distant points. We are, however, very much gratified, notwithstanding the inclemency of the weather, to see so many intelligent gentlemen present. I accept the position of temporary Chairman of this Convention, and would suggest the appointment of a Committee on Credentials and Permanent Organization, to report as early as our evening session.

While waiting your further pleasure, I would say that I feel, gentlemen, as though this is not an East Saginaw, or a Bay City, or a Saginaw City, or in fact, a Convention that has reference to any particular locality in this vicinity, but that is a *great national project*; one which, however, if carried out, will benefit certain localities on the line of this great national railway.

We have received letters from many distinguished gentlemen from different parts of the country, which may be read by the Secretary for your information.

We had hoped that we should secure the attendance of the delegation from our own State in Congress, as we look for aid from that quarter to help us build the Northern Pacific Railroad, and especially from the head of the lake down through Northern Michigan, and on further East, so as to connect with other contemplated lines.

I am sorry to say that for want of time we were obliged to defer the Convention so late as to bring us into quite a severe beginning of winter; at the same time could not call it earlier for want of time after the project was once thought of, to spread the invitations sufficiently wide.

You will permit me one suggestion : At the Convention that I recently had the honor to attend at Oswego, N. Y., the Convention was opened and closed with prayer. Whatever may be our individual opinion in regard to this, it is a respect that we owe to the sentiment of the community at large, and in accordance with a time-honored custom. At the request of a large number of delegates present, I will invite Dr. McCarty to open the Convention with prayer.

The Rev. Dr. McCarty thereupon invoked the divine blessing on the deliberations of the Convention.

Hon. Wm. Phelps, of Detroit, moved that a Committe of five be appointed to examine the credentials of Delegates, and report the names of those present who are entitled to seats in the Convention, which motion prevailed, and the Chair appointed as the

COMMITTEE ON CREDENTIALS,

W. H. Craig, of Detroit, J. A. Hubbell, of Houghton, C. K. Robinson, of East Saginaw, Hon. D. H Jerome, of Saginaw City, and Hon. Randolph Strickland of St. Johns.

J. A. Hubbell, of Houghton, moved that a Committee of five be appointed to report the names of Officers for the permanent organization of the Convention, which was carried, and the Chair appointed as the

COMMITTEE ON PERMANENT ORGANIZATION,

Hon. Wm. Phelps, of Detroit, H. M. Fitzhugh, of Bay City,

Hon. Eugene Pringle, of Jackson, Artemas Thayer, of Flint, and G. Morton, of Monroe.

The Chair announced that a number of letters and telegrams relating to the object of the Convention had been received from prominent gentlemen who were unable to attend in person; and with the permission of the meeting they should be read while the Convention was awaiting the reports of its Committees just appointed. The Secretary accordingly read the following:

TELEGRAM FROM THE MAYOR OF GRAND HAVEN.

GRAND HAVEN, Nov. 23, 1869.

To Hon. JAMES L. KETCHAM:

In any settled plan adopted in your Convention relating to the interest of Michigan and the Northern Pacific Railroad, the city of Grand Haven will concur. Local interests requiring my personal attention prevent my being with you.

DWIGHT CUTLER, *Mayor.*

LETTER FROM THE MAYOR OF OSWEGO, N. Y.

OSWEGO, Nov. 18, 1869.

Hon. JOHN F. DRIGGS,
      Dear Sir:
            I very much regret being unable to attend your Convention on the 23d inst. It is an important Convention and I wish you success.

I wish to introduce to you Mr. John A. Barry, Editor of the Daily *Palladium* of this city, with whom I think you became somewhat acquainted when here at our Convention. Mr. Barry is probably the only one of our delegation able to attend. He will represent us in a proper manner, and give a good account of the proceedings in his paper.

Very Truly Yours,
            A. S. PAGE.

LETTER FROM JAY COOKE.

PHILADELPHIA, Nov. 19, 1869.

Hon. JOHN F. DRIGGS,
      East Saginaw.
            Your favor of 15th inst is received. I must answer the questions proposed in your call very briefly, if at all. These questions number seventeen. I will take them in their order:

1st.   In my opinion there *is* immediate necessity for more railroads across the continent.   Two, at least; the Northern and Southern roads, should be begun at once and completed within three or four years.   If our Government expects the fealty of these vast regions, it should bind them to the East, and make the inhabitants of the territories and the Pacific States feel that they are a part of the United States, practically as well as in name.

2d.   I think the Northern Pacific Road secures a vast advantage by reaching water communication, which at the head of Lake Superior, is as near the Atlantic as Chicago is; but this advantage is only for a portion of the year, and does not apply to light freights or first class travel.   It does apply, however, to a vast trade in grain and other articles, and to emigrant travel

3d.   I do not consider it worth while to argue the comparative cost of railroad and water transportation.   There will be enough for all to do when the vast regions to the West and Northwest of Lake Superior are opened to settlement and cultivation.

4th.   If Canada belonged to us, we would soon cross the Sault Ste. Mary, skirt the north shore of Lake Huron, run down the Ottawa to Montreal, thence to Portland, thus making that city with Puget Sound; but as Canada is not ours, and not likely to be soon, Portland, as a terminus, is out of the question, and we cannot enter Canada at the Sault Ste. Mary.   The Northern Pacific, after touching the lake at the mouth of Montreal river, would seek the best route to the Straits of Mackinac.   Crowning these, it would seek an outlet by the various roads centering at Detroit, Toledo, etc.   Of course the road would send a portion of its business, *via* St. Paul, to Chicago, St. Louis, etc.

5th.   I am satisfied that, unless there are insurmountable difficulties at the Straits of Mackinac, any railroad seeking an eastern outlet *via* the south shore of Lake Superior and the Peninsula would find it to the advantage of the road to take this route.

6th.   I have answered this in my reply to the first question.

7th.   I do not think the Government should, at present, make direct grants of money or bonds for any purpose except for the ordinary river and harbor, and other similar objects, and other improvements.   But I do think that some plan should be devised whereby these great trans-continental improvements may be at once commenced and rapidly completed, and I am confident that aid can be given in such form as will not increase the public debt one dollar, or jeopardize the interests of the public treasury, and yet will be all-sufficient to secure the capital required.   Should such aid be granted, it should only be on condition that the Government should hold a first lien on the road franchises, lands and rolling stock.   This aid would be effectual if given in the form of an endorsement of guarantee of the principal and interest of the roads, and such plans could be adopted as would provide for the interest from the proceeds of bonds, so that the Government could not possibly be called upon to advance the funds for the interest for several years to come, if at all, for it may safely be assumed that, when finished, these roads will earn the full interest on their cost the first year.

8th, 9th and 10th. I send you a report just made by W. Milner Roberts. This report I do not desire published, as it is *not yet made public*, but it must unmistakably confirm all that has been said heretofore of the glorious character of the country along most of the route, and that tributary to the Northern Pacific Road.

11th. The North Pacific route, *via* Puget Sound, would shorten the distance to China, Japan, etc , over eight hundred miles.

12th. This question, of course, is answered by *all* in the affirmative.

13th. The national debt would be liquidated more rapidly by these enterprises becoming successful. The area of taxation would be greatly enlarged, and all parts of the nation would be invigorated and made stronger.

The remaining questions I must pass by, except a brief reference to the 17th and last. We who were born in the West, and have seen the wondrous progress of the last 40 years, *cannot* be too sanguine in our anticipations of the future glory of the North-West. I dare not trust my pen to foretell the future, as I expect to see it, should I live twenty years longer.

I regret that I have not time to do justice to the whole subject as contained in your questions. I hope the Convention will do what it can to influence Congress to grapple with the vital subject, and to enact such laws as will, while protecting the Government to the uttermost and not increasing the public debt, yet give effective and prompt aid to these enterprises.

Sincerely Yours,

JAY COOKE.

LETTERS FROM SENATOR HOWARD.

DETROIT, Nov. 7, 1869.

MY DEAR SIR: I am very glad to see the call for a Northern Pacific Railroad Convention, to be held at East Saginaw on the 23d inst. The time fixed is so near the commencement of the next session of Congress that I may be prevented from attending, though I should be right glad to be on hand.

The series of questions to be discussed are all extremely important. One more might be added, and I think it should be, viz.: What, if any, distance will be saved in running the road down our Upper Peninsula and across the Straits of Mackinac to the Eastern markets, rather than from the head of Lake Superior to Chicago? There is some dispute about this, and the question ought to be carefully and fully considered. My own idea is that the Mackinac route is considerably shorter. It is important, however, that the thing should be clearly verified, and not left to conjecture. You will at once see the importance of the question.

I might add another query—the practicability of running a train of cars across the Straits of Mackinac; but, as that is a pure question of civil engineering to be determined by scientific men, I would not add it. Mr. Johnson, the engineer of the N. P. R. R. Co., has often assured me that the thing is entirely practicable, and I believe him. He is a very sensible, well-instructed man. I am looking with great interest for his report to his Company of the surveys and explorations of the Company the past year.

As to a cash subsidy for this railroad, from Congress, I candidly think the idea had better be given up. If we grant a subsidy in bonds or indorsements to one Company, we must to another, and the railroad (Kansas Pacific) on the 35th degree and the famous Fremont line on the 32d degree—and Heaven knows what other lines of Pacific railroads—will assert their claims to the like aid from Government. The treasury can't stand this whole brood of suckers; their hunger would exhaust a world of subsidies. And this, you may rely, is the feeling. No more cash subsidies to railroads is, you may take it for granted, the sentiment of the people and of Congress.

You remember the omnibus bill reported by a majority of my committee in the Senate. Well, that bill is as " dead as a smelt." There is no chance of its passing whatever. It is dead and buried. The N. P. R. R. was provided for in that bill. I told Mr. Rice, Mr. Canfield, Mr Smith, and others interested in the Northern Pacific, that there was no chance of its passage; no, not at all.

But the Northern Pacific Company need not despair. They have their destinies in their own hands, and, with careful management, *can build the road* and make money. Their charter grants them (substantially) a strip of land 40 miles wide, across the continent from the western boundary of Minnesota, and 20 miles wide east of that line—land enough for an empire—more land, I believe, than is embraced in the State of New York—the most of which is rich and productive, covered with timber, full of other resources, and traversed by numerous navigable streams, facilities which, as everybody knows, do not exist upon the U. P. R. R , the Central P. R. R., of California, the Kansas P. R R , or the railroad on the 32d degree. Again, the U. P. and the Central (forming one line) pass over mountain ranges 8 000 feet above the level of the sea, and have to be "shedded" against snow slides, while there is no point where the Northern Pacific will pass a height more than 3,500 feet above the level of the sea This advantage in favor of the Northern route is inestimable.

As to the obstruction from snow along the Northern line, the testimony is conclusive that it will not be greater than on the roads through New England and Pennsylvania. The further you go West, on the same parallel of latitude, the milder the temperature becomes. This is physically proved by years of careful observation on the part of scientific men who have for long years wintered and summered in those regions. Why, Mr. Flanders, the recent delegate from Washington Territory, who resides on latitude between 46 and 47 in that Territory, told me, last session, that the peach, plum, cherry, Indian corn, and other products of the 41st to the 42d degree, all grow and mature in that climate as finely as in any other part of the world. I don't foresee much obstruction from snow and ice on that line—very little.

From Shanghai, in China, to Chicago, that route will be 500 miles shorter than by way of San Francisco. What a saving in transportation is here! Again, Puget Sound, the western terminus of the road, is the best harbor in the world. Any number of ships can take shelter there, no matter what their draft of water. And, with the exception of San Francisco, it is the only harbor worthy of the name from San Diego, the southern extremity of California, to Sitka, in Alaska.

But time would fail me to go into all the considerations to show the importance of this route to the Pacific, and I must close by expressing the conviction that within a few years it will be apparent to the whole world that it is the best route to the Pacific and to the East Indies across the continent.

The opinions which the Convention may enunciate will have great weight, and will, for good or evil, bear powerfully upon the pecuniary interests of that Company. They should be well considered, therefore, and founded upon firm data.

It is not to be denied that the States more immediately interested in this great work are Northern States—all New England, New York, Michigan, Wisconsin, Illinois, Minnesota, Iowa, Nebraska. The Territories of Dakotah, Montana, Idaho, Washington, all have a deep interest in the enterprise These communities are at least something in the scale of commerce and political power, and their voice, in both respects, is potent.

Yours truly,

Hon. John F. Driggs.   J. M. HOWARD.

Detroit, Nov. 21, 1869.

Dear Sir: Your answer to my former letter came early to hand. What I said about cash subsidies to railroads was advanced simply as my own opinion as to the future action of Congress, not as indicating what my own vote would be in a proper case. I ever thought, and still think, that the Northern Pacific Railroad is as deserving of such a subsidy as any line that has received it, and have labored hard, heretofore, to secure it for that road. If I could have my way in the matter, I certainly should extend the credit of the Government to that work, while I am not prepared to say the same of any other line that has been recently projected. I mean the lines named (with that line) in the Senate "Omnibus bill" of last session, because I see that the Northern route is to be, one day, the great route to the Pacific and the East Indies, and to give the people of this country a decided advantage even of the Suez Canal.

You are, of course, at liberty to make such use of my letters as you think best.

I should be very glad to attend the Convention, but as my children are all from home, and I am preparing to start for Washington, I find it extremely difficult to do so.

Very truly yours,

HON. JOHN F. DRIGGS.   J M. HOWARD.

<hr>

LETTER FROM GOVERNOR BALDWIN.

EXECUTIVE OFFICE,
DETROIT, November 22, 1869.

HON. JOHN F. DRIGGS, East Saginaw.

DEAR SIR: I am in receipt of your favor of Nov. 19, inviting me to attend a Railroad Convention at East Saginaw, on Tuesday, the 23d inst. I should certainly endeavor to be with you on that occasion but for the meeting of the various State Boards, at Lansing, on the morning of the 24th, which requires my presence at the capital at that time.

No other class of public improvements has done so much for the growth, advancement and prosperity of the country as the construction of railroads. I am not, however, one of those who advocate the building of railroads without regard to the character and value of the country from which they are to derive their support.

The natural advantages of Michigan are unsurpassed by those of any other State. I have for many years felt the importance of, and have advocated the construction of, a railroad through the center of the Lower Peninsula to the Straits of Mackinac, with east and west branches, from the vicinity of Houghton Lake to the Grand Traverse country on the west, and Thunder Bay on the east. Such a road would traverse a country of unsurpassed fertility of soil, and covered with a variety of timber of untold value. Yet the very fact of its being heavily timbered has thus far retarded such improvements in that section of the State, because of the somewhat increased cost of construction, and of the greater difficulty in bringing immediately into a state of cultivation land covered with a heavy growth of wood. Other causes have also operated to keep back the construction of railroads in the northern portion of our State ; these, however, are now being done away.

At the present time railroads are being built in almost every portion of the State, some of which are stretching out their arms towards the north.

The southern portion of the Lower Peninsula has, for a long time, had its three great lines running east and west—the Michigan Southern, the Michigan Central, and the Detroit & Milwaukee. From each of these are lines diverging both north and south to a reater or less extent.

Without pretending to name the many roads in operation, in process of construction, or projected, tending to the development of the State, there are some great trunk lines partially finished, in operation, and in progress of completion, which have a direct bearing upon the subject, to consider which the Convention has been specially called

The Flint & Pere Marquette, with its initial or starting point at Holly, on the Detroit & Milwaukee, on the eastern side of the State, already opened to Midland and to Bay City, and soon to be completed to Pere Marquette, or some other point on Lake Michigan—the Jackson, Lansing & Saginaw road, with its starting point at Jackson, in the center, already in operation to Saginaw and Wenona, and taking measures to continue its line to Houghton Lake and beyond—the Grand Rapids & Indiana Railroad, on the west, from the southern line of the State at Sturgis, already opened from Grand Rapids forty miles north, and steadily progressing towards Grand Traverse or the Straits of Mackinaw—these three great and most valuable lines of roads are steadily going forward.

From the vicinity of Houghton Lake north to the Straits of Mackinaw there should be but one road. Could all interests be united, and, with this union of strength, a single road be constructed from Houghton Lake to the Straits, with lateral branches to Lake Huron on the east and Traverse Bay on the west, it could not fail to result in the rapid development of the northern part of the State; population would flow in with a rapidity hitherto unknown, enriching the State and at the same time furnishing a large local traffic for the road.

So far I have alluded to the development of the southern peninsula only, but we should not overlook the resources of the northern peninsula, rich, almost beyond calculation, in its mineral wealth of iron and copper. Most wisely, in my judgment, the Constitution prohibits the State from being interested in any work of internal improvement, or carrying on any such work, except in the expenditure of grants to the State of lands or other property. It is not necessary, to secure the construction of these roads, that the State should undertake the work. Congress has made large appriations of lands for this purpose. These lands, already valuable, will greatly appreciate by the construction of the roads.

Our country is yet in its infancy. Population is flowing to us, from every part of the world, with wonderful rapidity. One great line of railway already unites the Atlantic with the Pacific. Another shorter and better line, the Northern Pacific, is also to be constructed. It is simply a question of time, and no people can be more deeply interested in the adoption of this line than the citizens of Michigan It is not necessary to oppose connections between the Northern Pacific road and Chicago, but, whatever may be its connection with other lines around the south end of Lake Michigan, it should be the policy of the Government to make the line, as far as possible, through the undeveloped portions of the country, and especially so if that country is, as in this case, of valuable character and capable of sustaining a large and dense population; and still further, when such line would shorten the distance to the large manufacturing States of New England, and to Europe from the sea-board.

Every consideration would seem to favor the construction of a road through Northern Michigan, and making that road a part of the line of the great Northern Pacific.

I trust that the deliberations of the convention will tend to hasten the construction of the road through both peninsulas of our noble commonwealth, and to further the undertaking and completion of the great practical northern line to the Pacific coast.

Sincerely regretting my inability to participate with you in the proceedings of the convention, I am,

Very respectfully yours,
H P. BALDWIN.

LETTER FROM HON. JOHN A. POOR.

PORTLAND, Nov. 18, 1869.

HON. JAS. L. KETCHAM, Mayor of East Saginaw, and others.

GENTLEMEN : I have the honor to acknowledge the receipt of your invitation to attend a convention, at your city, on the 23d inst., of those friendly to the contemplated line of the Northern Pacific Railroad "from the head of Lake Superior, by the way of the Straits of Mackinac " and across the State of Michigan, to a point of connection with the line of the proposed trans-continental railway from the St. Clair river to Portland, Halifax, and the most eastern shore of Newfoundland, and regret that prior indispensable engagements compel me to forego the pleasure of a visit, at this time, to your interesting section of the country.

In this connection it gives me pleasure to inform you that a section of the European and North American Railway, 80 miles in length, between the River St. Johns, at St. Johns city, and the River St. Croix, the eastern boundary of the United States, is to be formally opened for business on the 1st of December—at which opening I hope to be present—leaving but 56 miles of unfinished line, now in rapid progress, between Bangor and St. Johns city, the entire line from Halifax to Bangor being all in progress, to be opened through, 600 miles from Portland to Halifax, during the year 1870.

Portland and Saginaw are upon the same parallel of latitude, and the deflection from an air line to Portland, which you are compelled to make to pass Lake Huron, is scarcely sufficient to be taken into account in projecting a great line of railway to the sea-board.

We all recognize Chicago as the present great commercial point in the Northwest, but any one must perceive, on reference to a map, the extraordinary advantages for a great city at the head of

Lake Superior, and it is apparent to any one that, from the head of Lake Superior to the foot of Lake Huron, the shortest practicable route will be found by the Straits of Mackinac, resorting to a ferry to connect the two sections of such a line.

The interesting manner in which the claims of the enterprise were presented to the Oswego convention by its President, the Hon. John F. Driggs, for many years your able and honored Representative in Congress, with the aid of the great map present at that convention, produced a decided and profound impression, and while the call for the Oswego convention looked mainly for a line from Portland to Chicago, we could not fail to see that the great Northwest, lying far above Chicago, was ultimately to be reached from the Atlantic sea-board, by the direct line contemplated by your call, to the head of Lake Superior by the Straits of Mackinac.

I will not attempt to describe the present value or the mighty future of the vast interior, which will naturally connect itself by rail with the head of Lake Superior, lying upon both sides of the boundary line. But there is a vast, unoccupied region, destined in the future to sustain as dense a population as that which now inhabits the same latitudes on the Eastern Continent, in Northern Europe and Asia, and the testimony shows that wheat can be raised as far north as the 60th degree of latitude, and Indian corn over a portion of this region of the vast and well watered table lands west and northwest of Lake Superior.

I had occasion, in a memorial to the Legislature of Canada, in 1854, to say " that from the shore of the Atlantic ocean, at Portland, to the head waters of the Missouri river, every portion of the country presents the greatest possible attractions to invite immigration ; that a mild climate, healthy at all seasons of the year, a soil of abundant fertility for the production of food, with rich mines and luxuriant forests, are here found for the hundreds of miles beyond the head of Lake Superior, if not to the base of the Rocky Mountains.

" If the waters of these mighty rivers could be turned into Lake Superior, and be at the same time made navigable to the sea, we might form some idea of the value and importance of a railroad from Portland to the head of Lake Superior, and to the region of country beyond it.

" The distance from the great bend of the Missouri, by railway, to the Atlantic ocean, at Portland, would be hundreds of miles less than by following the Mississippi and Missouri rivers to their mouth at New Orleans." .

Engaged as you are in the carrying out of a most important section of a great national and international work, I cannot fail to express my hearty sympathy in your labors, and my wishes for its abundant success. Very respectfully,
Your obedient servant,
JOHN A. POORE.

LETTER FROM THE VICE-PRESIDENT OF THE R., W. & O. R. R.

ROME, WATERTOWN & OGDENSBURG RAILROAD, ⎱
VICE-PRESIDENT'S OFFICE, ⎰
NEW YORK, Nov. 16th, 1869.

HON. JOHN F. DRIGGS,

DEAR SIR: I received, a few days since, a circular letter, under your frank, inviting me to attend a Railroad Convention to be held at East Saginaw on the 23d.

I have delayed answering till now, that I might be able to state definitely whether it would be possible for me to be present, and am now obliged to say that I must forego that pleasure. From the number and variety of topics to be presented for consideration, I conclude that the meeting is for the discussion of railroad extension generally; doubtless, however, intended to have a special reference to a few particular projects named in the circular.

The general question of railroad extension is one in which I feel a deep interest. Taking the large view, and not being confined to those projects that are in, or tending in, the direction of the road with which I am connected, I have had an opportunity to observe some very marked instances of roads which have been undertaken, and finally completed under great difficulties, into new sections, where the construction of a road, at all, was regarded by many as impracticable, and by others as premature, but I have lived to see the immense benefits, at first confined to the country traversed by the road, in a very few years reflected back again to the road, and the capital employed in its construction returned *with good interest.*

As far as I am informed, I am inclined to believe the route in which you are, I think, particularly interested, is not dissimilar from the instances named, with this advantage in its favor: That to local earnings, which must be large, derived from the whole of Northern Michigan, now only needing such an inlet and outlet to make it equal to any other section of the State,—to this will be added a large through traffic from the Superior region, and especially from the head of that lake and proximate to it, already becoming the greatest wheat producing region in the West, and also from the connections that will be made with other roads, and especially with the "Northern Pacific," which may be counted upon, with great certainty, to be constructed within a very few years. For myself, I regard the inducements to the capitalist, and to the General Government to undertake this work, as far greater, in every point of view, than was the case in regard to the Pacific road, already built, when it was projected.

Great and extended as our American railway system has already become, it is but the beginning of that which we shall behold in the near future. We shall also witness equally great changes in the adaptation not only of the roads themselves, but of the equipment and management of the same, tending to a more general use of this system. It is now rapidly overcoming, and soon to defy, competition with any and all other means of transportation of property, as it has already done in the conveyance of persons.

It cannot be doubted, so far as the area of land is concerned, as well as the perfect adaptation of soil and climate, that we are now able to supply the world with bread and the other elements of food dependant on the soil for production. The only obstacle that can be discerned to our doing so is the one contingent upon the cost of transportation from the field to the points of distribution. That this is to be accomplished by the roads built, and to be built, cannot be doubted Every other question affecting the future growth, greatness and prosperity of our great "Empire of the West" sinks into utter insignificance as compared with this, which applies equally to the districts in which cotton, sugar, tobacco and rice, the great *American staples*, are produced.

I must not ask your attention longer to what might be added upon a question of such interest ; and again regretting that I cannot meet yourself and other railroad men at the convention, which, I trust, may result in accomplishing all that is expected,

I am very truly yours, etc.,

MARCELLUS MASSEY.

LETTER FROM HON. JOHN NEAL.

PORTLAND, MAINE, 13th Nov., 1869.

To JAMES L. KETCHAM, Esq., Mayor of East Saginaw, and his Associates of the Common Council.

GENTLEMEN : I have delayed answering your invitation till to-day, hoping so to arrange my business that I could be with you and assist in your deliberations ; but as I find now that I cannot do this, allow me to send you a few words of congratulation and encouragement.

On looking at the map, to which you call our attention, I find unquestionable indications of that same providential foresight which buried all the treasures of earth at the beginning—all our precious metals, our gems, our anthracite, our bituminous coal and our peat, as well as our iron, our lead, our zinc and our marbles— at a depth exactly corresponding to our necessities, our growth and our energy, obliging us to inquire after them and to *dig for* them, just as our agricultural riches have to be dug for, and are always found just *where* and *when* they are most needed.

Just so has it ever been, and is now, with our magnificent railroad enterprises. When they are wanted, they are always found. The signs are all along our pathway, and are always *cropping out*, like our mineral treasures, only to be overlooked till they are wanted. And what is more, when we go to the map, after due consideration, we find our boldest undertakings foreshadowed there by the very lay of the land, so that we begin to wonder why they have never been thought of before.

The mountains and rivers testify for your encouragement, just as in Maryland and Pennsylvania; iron and coal, and lime for the flux, with sand for the furnace, are found lying side by side, for hundreds of miles upon a stretch, overhung by a wilderness of growing charcoal, and all to be had, if not for the asking, certainly for the digging and chopping, the burning and blasting.

Under this view, the map you refer to is of itself a prophecy. You find a way left open to you from the beginning of the world ; a pathway for nations over seas and continents.

Ten years ago the road you have in view was not *wanted*. Had your magnificent scheme been projected then, it would have been a dead failure, not for a season, only, but perhaps for generations. And why ? Because it was not then *needed*, and being attempted too early, the failure would have discouraged your posterity—like the enterprise of Darien ; it would have been postponed indefinitely, as being both visionary and preposterous.

Fifty years ago the golden treasure-house of California would not have been reached, though *dug for*. The time had not arrived. But now, when all the long-buried riches of our earth are honestly wanted, and whole communities are bestirring themselves, they are found cropping out everywhere along the highways of commerce, and always just where they are most needed and are most faithfully and steadfastly inquired after and *dug for*.

Just so will it be with your projected railway from Puget Sound to the harbor of Portland, Maine   It is now *wanted*, and the want is felt, from the Atlantic to the Pacific, as a great necessity, alike unappeasable and active.   Can there be a doubt, then, of its triumphant and early success ?   Look at the map once more, and see if you do not find there all the encouragement you need.   I have called it a prophecy.   It is more ; it is a poem, a magnificent epic, where the machinery of two worlds must soon be employed.   You may see all this, if so disposed, in the evident provision therein made for the fulfilment of the vast undertaking you have now entered upon.

But you, gentlemen, are business men ; you have come together for business—you *mean business ;* and I have only to add that, in my judgment, the future is full of promise for you, and that the sooner you sink your shafts, and the sooner your furnaces are in blast for smelting the ore committed to your charge, the sooner you will understand what the Builder of the Universe had in view when He laid out this magnificent highway for you, through mountain ranges and over rivers—over seas and continents, rather—for such it will be in time, and long before this generation has been gathered to its fathers.

Wishing you the success you so well deserve, and I could not well say more, I am, gentlemen, your friend and fellow-laborer,
                              JOHN NEAL.

GRAND HAVEN, Nov. 17, 1869.

GENTLEMEN : I with pleasure acknowledge the receipt of a printed call and letter inviting attention to, and presence at, a convention to be held at East Saginaw on the 23d inst., looking to a speedy completion of the Northern Pacific and Michigan Short Line Railroad. Unavoidable public duties, I regret to say, will prevent the possibility of my being present.

The call has been published in the papers of this city, and the attention of the Common Council thereof invited to the subject

I need not say that the project meets my cordial approval, for no one identified with the growth and prosperity of Michigan could lend other than hearty co-operation.

Trusting that the convention, in the consideration of the vast interests involved, may arrive at some possible plan by which it will be made to appear that the trans-continental railroad, via the Northern Pacific and Straits of Mackinac route, is not only the shortest one from the Pacific to the Atlantic sea-boards, but a route thoroughly practicable, I join you in lively hopes for the completion of this great national highway.

I have the honor to be, very respectfully,

Your obedient servant,

T. W. FERRY.

HON. JAMES L. KETCHAM, *Mayor*, and others.

DRYDEN, LAPEER Co., MICH., ⎱
Nov. 28th, 1869.   ⎰

HON. JOHN F. DRIGGS, East Saginaw, Mich.

DEAR SIR : Your note of invitation, and circular, is received, and contents noted.

The object of the convention, as set forth in your circular, is one of vital importance to the people of this State, and more particularly to those of the Upper Peninsula and that portion of the State you had the honor to represent in the Congress of the United States.

I have conversed with quite a number of the leading men in the eastern part of our county, and their voice is as that of one man. They regard the enterprise as second to no one of its kind in the nation, and one that must, from the very nature of circumstances, be ultimately a success.

One thing is morally certain—that the Saginaw Valley will be on the line of the proposed road, and whether Detroit or Port Huron should be the next point of importance in the State touched by this great national artery, the result will be about the same, so

far as benefiting Northern Michigan   Still the people in this locality would be more directly interested in a road that would make
Detroit one of its objective points.

I regret very much that circumstances beyond my control forbid
my being present at the convention.

We shall look forward, with a great deal of interest, to the result
of this very important gathering in your city, and with a hope
based upon the best of reasons, shall look forward to the ultimate
and final triumph of all you propose.

I am, dear sir,
Yours, very respectfully,
L. KENDRICK.

LETTER FROM HON. WM. E. DICKINSON.

MICHIGAN EXCHANGE, }
DETROIT, Nov. 9th, 1869.

HON. JOHN F. DRIGGS, East Saginaw.

DEAR SIR: As I passed through Milwaukee yesterday P. M., I
noticed that it was intended to call a Railroad Convention in your
city in regard to railroads in Upper Michigan. Will you please
send a circular of the proposed meeting to Robert H. Larnborn,
Esq., Secretary Lake Superior & Mississippi Railroad, Fifth
and Library streets, Philadelphia, Pa.

I shall try and be present myself.

With kindest regards to yourself,

Truly yours,
WM. E. DICKINSON,
54 William street,
(Room 26,)
New York.

LETTER FROM EDGAR CONKLING, ESQ.

DETROIT, MICHIGAN, Nov. 15, 1869.

HON. JOHN F. DRIGGS :

DEAR SIR: I am now on my way to Sheboygan, Michigan,
where I shall be for the present and until I can build at Mackinaw
City the coming spring. I went to Ohio in 1829, and to Cincin-
nati in 1841, and now come to your State to reside for the balance
of my life, and propose developing my property at the Straits of
Mackinaw, of some 35,000 acres, in accordance with the plan set
forth in my pamphlet sent you. But for the lateness of the season,
I would gladly attend your coming Railroad Convention, on the
23d, at Saginaw, of great interest to your State and whole country.

I began to urge the construction of railroads to and from the
Straits, on either side, in all directions, in 1853, and then secured
Old Mackinaw, foreseeing the day would come when there would

be an important union of rail and water lines of commerce. I have fully posted myself in regard to all that country, and I challenge the refutation of my assertion that there is no point·on the northern lakes surrounded with so many elements of manufacturing, and that its agricultural capabilities are greatly underrated, and that the construction of railroads through that section of country to Superior City will develop more latent wealth, in a few years, than that of the settled portion of the southern peninsula of Michigan. No such agricultural and mineral country, with such cheap facilities of transportation for distribution, while on the high road of the most important line between Europe and Asia, can fail to become a populous and wealthy country—much more so than other sections now being settled, much less favored with such elements and proximity to market.

The Northern Pacific Railroad will need all the outlets possible to get, whether by water from Superior City, or by railroad *via* St. Paul and Chicago, or Detroit *via* Mackinaw. No selfish ideas should be allowed in this great national highway. All sections of the country contributing to its aid should equally share in its benefits. The short time limited for its construction suggests the greatest harmony in prosecuting the work and in securing needed legislation. For one, I shall seek to present Northern Michigan to the public in a manner that will invite greater attention to its many superior advantages for manufacturing and commerce.

Yours respectfully,
EDGAR CONKLING.

LETTER FROM HENRY STEPHENS, ESQ.

ALMONT, Nov. 20, 1869.

MR. A. P. BREWER, East Saginaw.

DEAR SIR : I understand there is to be a Railroad Convention at your city on the 22d. I do not think any of our people will be there, and therefore have been requested to write some one who will take the trouble to inform those interested that we, the towns of Almont and Dryden, wish to be on the route adopted to reach the Michigan Air Line Railroad, as we have been informed it is one of the objects of the convention to take measures to organize a company to make such connection, and we would suggest if the road goes to Lapeer, that as Armada is the most northern point on the Michigan Air Line, and the topography of the country between Lapeer and Armada is very level, and no streams to cross, of any size, that this route, being direct, is no doubt the cheapest to build, and can and will raise the greatest amount of aid. I am confident that Almont and Dryden would by vote and subscription raise $100,000 to $150,000, and we want to have the chance to do it. Try and advocate our claims, and you will have our thanks.

Perhaps the best way would be to place this letter in the hands of those who are active and influential in this enterprise, and you can vouch for the writer, I trust, and can also give any information as to feasibility of route.

Very truly yours,
HENRY STEPHENS.

At the conclusion of the reading of the letters, the President said :

If it is the pleasure of the Convention, I will occupy some of its time now in reading a paper that I have prepared myself, more especially with reference to the wealth and probable advantages to be secured to a line in the northern portion of our State. I have prepared the paper at the request of gentlemen of the committee, and I do not wish to intrude upon the Convention now, unless it is their pleasure.

A motion was made and carried that the President proceed now with his report, as proposed. Mr. Driggs then read the following :

PAPER READ BY MR. DRIGGS.

GENTLEMEN OF THE CONVENTION : Within the last few years we have witnessed the marvelously rapid construction of one railroad line from ocean to ocean, across the center of the United States. This road was commenced during the rebellion, was prosecuted through a terrible war for its suppression, and completed soon after its close; an achievement, under the circumstances, which no other nation ever equalled ; a triumph, within the time, of engineering, of labor, and perseverance, to which the history of the world furnishes no parallel.

The *present* needs two more Pacific railroads, a Northern and a Southern road ; and the rapidly approaching future *will have them.* What has been done, under more favorable circumstances, certainly can be done again.

The Government made very large grants of land to the Union and Central roads, and also to the Northern Pacific—the charter to which grants forty sections to the mile from the western boundary of Minnesota, and twenty sections east of that line to the head of Lake Superior. In a letter from the Hon. J. M. Howard, U. S. Senator, he computes this grant to be equal in extent to the State of New York ; being a strip across the continent nearly forty miles wide. The greater portion of this vast area of land is unsurpassed in richness of soil, timber and minerals, and highly favored by the even mildness of its climate ; yet, without access by means of a railroad, is comparatively without value. Most of it would remain undisposed of at $1 25 per acre, and unoccupied under the homestead or pre-emption laws for many years in the future. But build the road, and all the arable lands within the limits, and other portions valuable for minerals and timber, would be rapidly taken up by actual settlers, and considered cheap at ten times their present value.

The land grant to the Union and Central Pacific roads is believed to be far less valuable than the Northern Pacific grant, by reason of the extended barren plains, the wider mountain ranges of much greater altitude, the deeper winter snows, and the inferiority and severity of the climate on the line over which the roads pass. It cannot be denied, however, that these roads are (for the immediate present) compensated for this deficiency by the fact that their western terminus is at the present populous Pacific metropolis, San Francisco, and that they pass through many intermediate towns and settlements, thus securing an immediate large amount of local traffic and travel. Portions of their lands, however, since the roads are built, are very valuable, while before the consummation of the great work they were entirely insufficient to secure the building of the roads, and might have remained so for fifty years to come

A Government subsidy, then, was necessary to secure the accomplishment of the work. The aid was given, and now the iron horse steams his way in seven days (one-eighth of the distance around the globe) from ocean to ocean, across a continent, over rivers and streams, through valleys and gorges, and over mountain tops eight thousand feet above the level of the sea. If these roads were a necessity, and if the Government acted wisely in extending its aid beyond that afforded by the land grant to the Central and Union Pacific, may it not be wise, also, to extend it to the Northern Pacific, and even to a Southern Pacific road?

From Shanghai to London, via Puget Sound, Lake Superior, Mackinaw and Portland, it is considerably nearer than via San Francisco and New York, with a much lighter grade; the highest point reached by the Northern Pacific road being, I believe, according to recent surveys, only about 3,500 feet above the level of the sea; while, as before remarked, the other road passes over an elevation of 8,000 feet.

The beauty and capacity of the harbor of Puget Sound, the western terminus of the Northern Pacific Railroad, are too well known to need any further praise. It is the finest harbor in the world.

The road from this magnificent haven to water communication with the Atlantic, at the head of Lake Superior, will be only 1,600 or 1,700 miles long; where the chain of rivers, lakes and canals, from the Gulf of St. Lawrence and New York, meets the road at Superior Bay, 1,500 miles from the Atlantic tide-water, and nearly half way across the continent at its widest point. Such an advantage as this unparalleled water-course affords for freight and traffic for seven months in the year, no other route across the continent can ever possess. It is not my purpose to furnish accurate tables

of comparative distances to show the saving in favor of the Northern Pacific over other routes from China to Europe, or from the
Pacific to Chicago, New York, Boston or Portland. These are
facts to be determined and settled by scientific men, by engineers,
and by exact computation of curves, angles, and distances. But
that is shorter it is evident, and that it is to become the great future
highway of travel and trade between Europe and Eastern Asia, no
man can doubt who properly appreciates the advantages of short
lines and of direct water communication between London and Paris
and the Northern Pacific Railroad at Superior Bay.

Independent of these great advantages for securing international
commerce and travel, the Northern Pacific route is far superior to
all others on account of the climate, productiveness of the soil,
timber, minerals, the rivers, streams, and the water facilities afforded on the line. It is of some of these I design more particularly
to speak, especially of the Northern Michigan and Mackinaw
route.

It has long since been demonstrated by experience that wheat,
barley, oats, hops, and all cereal productions, the potato, cabbage,
beet, turnip, and other like vegetables, as well as apples, pears,
plums, and some other fruits, grow more abundantly and are of
better quality in the highest latitudes where they can mature, than
in more southerly regions. For the production of most of these
articles, especially the great staple of wheat, the vast basin or region
of country lying between latitudes 44 and 54 north and longitudes
15 and 35 west from Washington, and known as the Saskatchewan,
the Red River of the North and Upper Missouri river valleys, is
unequalled by any other same number of acres upon the surface of
the earth.

This region alone, (through the center of which the road is to
pass,) when fully developed, is capable of supplying the world with
grain, and of sustaining fifty millions of souls, a number much
greater than the present population of the United States.

Of the timber, minerals, and soil upon the western slope, from
the summit of the dividing mountain range to Puget Sound, in
passing, I will only say that the testimony of all who have traveled
over the route, and are familiar with the country bordering the
same, is that its richness in these respects is only excelled by the
grazing and wheat growing qualities of the eastern slope, from the
mountains to Lake Superior.

Having thus far considered the subject from a general point of
view, and having briefly referred to the country and its productive
capabilities from Lake Superior to Puget Sound, I come now to
consider the question as to the route the road should take from the
head of Lake Superior to the Atlantic sea-board. From the head
of Lake Superior to Montreal river, the dividing line between
Michigan and Wisconsin, it is about 95 miles, and from that point
to Mackinaw about 275 miles—making the distance from Superior
to Mackinaw 370 miles, from Mackinaw to Saginaw 175 miles,

from Saginaw to Detroit 96 miles, from Saginaw river to St. Clair river, on a line to Lewiston or Niagara, 80 miles ; making the entire distance from Superior to Saginaw 545 miles, to Detroit 641, and to St. Clair river 625 miles. These distances, though not accurately determined by measurement, are believed to be substantially correct.

A road over this line, to connect at Lewiston with the one contemplated from Portland, must make a saving of distance, from Superior to that city, of about 200 miles over the route from Superior *via* Chicago. I am aware that this saving of distance will be diminished by a branch from the Northern Pacific, at some point considerably west of Superior, to Chicago; but Superior being the present eastern terminus fixed in the charter of the Northern Pacific for that road, and that being the great water outlet to the ocean, in summer, and the Mackinaw route offering the only competing railroad line for the shipment of the products of this vast northern region, it is of the greatest importance to the people of the same that this road should be built, even if the distance were no less than by Chicago.

The amount of local business that would be secured to such a road in Northern Michigan and Wisconsin, between Superior and the Saginaw river, seems to be but little understood or appreciated by the country, and I now desire to call the attention of this Convention and the railroad men of the East to the facts.

In the year 1835, or 1836, the Government of the United States (to settle the boundary dispute between Ohio and Michigan) ceded the Territory now known as the Upper Peninsula to the then Territory of Michigan. At this time, and for many years thereafter, very little was known of this important and valuable region, except that it was covered with timber and that copper had been discovered on Isle Royale and in some other localities, but as to the amount, or extent of its existence, no one knew. Nor is the value of its vast deposits of iron and copper known or appreciated even to this day.

As far back as 1636 copper was discovered by the Jesuit missionaries upon Lake Superior, and an attempt was made, in 1770, by an English company, to mine it. A vessel of 40 tons was built by this company upon Lake Superior, above the Sault, to transport men, machinery and supplies. Mining operations were commenced and prosecuted about two years near Ontonagon, but proving unprofitable, were abandoned in 1774.

The first scientific exploration of the mineral lands of Lake Superior was made by Dr. Douglass Houghton, Michigan State Geologist, between the years 1840 and 1845. He made annual reports of his discoveries, but as he perished, while prosecuting his labors, in 1845, by drowning, he never published his final report. The publication of his annual statements brought many to the district as early as 1843, and from that period to the present, copper mining has been pursued at many points on Lake Superior, and with varied successes, profits and losses.

Previous to this time, the entire freighting business of Lake Superior was carried on by one or two small schooners, which had to be built above the Sault. These rapids, in St. Mary's river, between Lakes Huron and Superior, are about one mile in length, and effectually prevented vessels from passing, by water, from the lower to the upper lake   In consequence of this, tram-ways were constructed around the falls, and several steamers hauled over the portage.

This slow and expensive process was rendered necessary, as no other means existed for obtaining vessels upon Lake Superior until the completion of the Sault Canal in 1855. That magnifient public work was built by the State of Michigan, through the aid of a grant of 750,000 acres of land made by the Government to the State, in 1853, for that purpose. At the period of the completion of the canal, and the free and uninterrupted passage of the largest vessels to and from Lake Superior, an immense impulse was given to the production and shipment of copper and iron. Before that time the expense of exportation made the production of these valuable minerals from their inexhaustible mines comparatively small. But, in the next eight years, as the following table will show, there was shipped from Lake Superior over $10,000,000 worth of copper alone :

	TONS.	POUNDS.
1855	7,642	
1855 t > 1857	11,312	
1858	3,500	
1859	4,200	
1860	6,000	
1861	7,400 ,	
1862	9,062	
1863	8,548	
1864	8,472	
1865	10,790	,,156
1866	10,375	1,68 '
1867	11,735	552
Total	90,037	1,396

This, as before remarked, brought in the market over $40,000,000; the product of 1867 bringing $4,700,000. During the present year (1869) there has been shipped from the Marquette Iron District about 600,000 tons of iron ore and pig metal, valued at $4,200,000.* The interest of copper has been greatly depressed, for the last few years, by the increased cost of production and for the want of as equal a protection as has been afforded to other similar interests. Under the protection now secured, it is hoped and believed that its production will increase until it shall reach an amount equal to the home demand, of fifteen or sixteen thousand tons per annum.

* For the actual product of the Marquette Iron District, in 1869, see letter from Hiram A. Burt, Esq., in Appendix to this pamphlet.

With the increased facilities which the Northern Pacific Railroad will afford for a winter shipment of these articles, and for taking in supplies of all kinds for their production, there can be no reasonable doubt of such a result, nor that the annual production of pig iron and iron ore will be increased to 800,000 instead of 600,000 tons, as at present. When this shall be done, the annual exports of iron and copper will be twelve or thirteen million dollars.

About one-half of the iron is brought from the mountains to Marquette over the Marquette Railroad, and shipped from that point, the other half being taken to Escanaba, at the head of Green Bay, over the Escanaba Railroad, and shipped from there. The copper is principally shipped from Ontonagon, Houghton, Hancock, Eagle River, Eagle Harbor, Copper Harbor, Lac La Belle and Torch Lake. Marquette, Negaunee, Houghton, Hancock and Rockland are populous towns. Marquette and Negaunee, in the iron district, and Houghton and Hancock, in the copper, containing about 4,000 inhabitants each, and for schools, churches, hotels, stores and dwellings, will compare favorably with other towns of the same size. The whole population of the Upper Peninsula is believed to be not far from 60,000.

The number of vessels which passed through the Sault Canal in 1864 was 1,414, their united tonnage being 571,183. These vessels, forming regular lines between Buffalo, Cleveland, Detroit, Milwaukee and Chicago, were about one-quarter large class steamers, the balance being sailing vessels. The immense stores of all descriptions freighted through the canal to supply the mines and these inhabitants are purchased from the merchants, mechanics and traders of Pittsburg, Cleveland, Buffalo, Detroit, Chicago and Milwaukee, and are paid for in copper, iron ore, pig iron, lath, shingles, etc. Not only do the lake cities have the benefit of the profits on these supplies, but the copper and iron received in exchange gives employment to thousands of their mechanics, artisans, and laborers in their smelting works, foundries and machine shops, and from which other large direct and indirect profits are derived. In fact, it is doubtful whether there is any other source from which they receive so great a benefit.

The Upper Peninsula of Michigan can never become, to any great extent, an agricultural region, that portion bordering on the lake being too rocky and the soil too poor for many kinds of crops. In some portions of it, however, farming may hereafter be profitably pursued. Grass, cabbage, turnips, beets, and several other vegetables, grow to perfection. Wheat, oats and barley also ripen there, while potatoes of the best quality grow in great abundance. In September last, I saw some very fine apples, pears and plums growing on the farms of Messrs. Sayles, Mercer and Cash, at Ontonagon, and the vegetables spoken of in their gardens, as well as on the land of Mr. Hoyt, at Rockland. None of these, however, yet grow in sufficient quantities for home consumption except potatoes, which are beginning to be exported. There is, however,

another source of wealth in the forests of white pine timber growing there; this, in consequence of its rapid exhaustion in all other
sections of the country, is soon to become second in value to the
mineral deposits.

So important has the Government of the United States considered the present and future products and commerce of Lake Superior to the country, that it has, from time to time, made large grants
of land and money to deepen its rivers. and to build its ship canals,
wagon and railroads. The principal grants for these objects have
been as follows: For the Sault Canal, 750,000 acres; for the Portage Lake Ship Canal, 400,000 acres; for the Lac La Belle Canal,
100,000 acres; for the Marquette and Ontonagon Railroad, about
640,000 acres; for the Escanaba and Negaunee Railroad, about
320,000 acres; for the Chicago and Northwestern Railroad about
326,000 acres, and for the Fort Howard and Copper Harbor wagon
road about 320,000 acres—making a total of appropriations of
2,856,000 acres of public lands. Of these, only about 1,600,000
acres have been actually acquired by the companies; 400,000 more
for the Portage Lake and Lake Superior Ship Canal Company
doubtless soon will be. The remaining 856,000 acres, for the west
half of the Marquette and Outonagon Railroad, from Lake Michi-
gaunee to Ontonagon, for the Northwestern Railroad, from Menominee to Escanaba, and for the military wagon road from the Wisconsin State line to Fort Wilkins, at Copper Harbor. will soon
revert to the Government, unless the grants are renewed. The
money appropriated and recommended has been: For a break-
water at Marquette, $250,000; for Ontonagon harbor, $200,000,
and for Eagle Harbor, $87,000—making $537,000. Besides this,
large sums have been appropriated for the St. Mary's river, for
light-houses, surveys, etc.

It has been carefully estimated, from as reliable data as can be
ascertained, that the annual production of white pine lumber in the
State of Michigan, including timber, shingles, and other descriptions, is greater than that produced in all the other States com-
bined, and that there is still standing in its forests a larger amount,
of a superior quality, than in all of the other territory east of the
Rocky Mountains. This quality of pine, once growing in New
York, Maine, and other eastern sections, has nearly all disappeared,
leaving Michigan, Wisconsin and Minnesota to supply the present
and rapidly increasing demand.

This almost indispensable and valuable timber once removed, is
never to be replaced, at least to any extent; for if allowed to grow
again, which is not the case, it would require from 50 to 80 years
to become as fully grown as at present.

Fifteen years ago the amount of lumber manufactured in the
State was, as compared with the present, very small. I am informed
by Mr. Curtis Emerson, one of the earliest lumbermen here, that

the only cargo of lumber shipped from the Saginaw Valley in 1846, twenty-three years ago, was on the schooner "Julia Smith," and consisted of 61,000 feet.

The following table will show the amount cut in the Valley in 1863, and the increase from that year to 1868, inclusive :

	FEET.
1863....	133,500,000
1864	215,000,000
1865	250,039,340
1866	349,787,884
1867	423,993,190
1868	457,396,225
Total	1,830,266,639

It has been ascertained that in the year 1868 there was cut, in the entire State, 1,600 000,000 feet, Saginaw Valley and the Bay Shore producing about one-third of the whole amount. Making what I suppose to be a low estimate, that the *annual* production in the whole State, in the last eighteen years, has been 400,000,000 feet, the entire product within that period has been 7,200,000,000 feet. Placing the average yield at 3,750 feet to the acre, and at 300,000 feet to the 80-acre lot, we find the enormous number of 1,920,' 00 acres from which the pine has been removed in this State.

Estimating the entire amount yet standing in Northern Michigan, including the Upper Peninsula at double the amount, say 4,000,000 acres, the future yield will be 15,000,000,000 feet, and at the present price of $15 per M , will be worth in market $225,-000,000. The timber, shingles, etc., will bring at least $75,-000,000 more, making the pine in the forests of Northern Michigan produce the vast sum of $300,000,000. This 4,000,000 acres of standing pine, at present rates of exhaustion, will all be cleared in 12 or 14 years. But as heretofore the pine has been mostly cut on streams accessible for running logs, and as much of the remaining timber, both in the Lower and the Upper Peninsula, is found in sections too distant from the water-courses to make them available for that purpose, the supply from such localities must depend upon future railroad and other facilities for transportation to market. Until such means are afforded, the annual yield must soon be diminished, and this may prolong the entire exhaustion of white pine in the State for a period of 18 or 20 years ; but beyond that, it is hardly possible.

Should the Northern Pacific Railroad be continued to Mackinac it will be about 2,000 miles long, and should its bonds be guaranteed by the Government for $30,000 per mile, (near the probable cost,) the entire guarantee would be $60,000,000, or one-fifth only of the value of the product of the pine forests of Northern Michigan.

The value of other timber can hardly be over-estimated, it being certain that no State in the Union has a larrger amount of white oak, maple, beech, ash, and other qualities of hard and soft timber, than Michigan. Of the article of oak staves there was manufactured and shipped from the Saginaw Valley alone in the year 1868:

6,846,000, which, at $60 per M., brought..	$ 410,760
The hard wood timber of all kinds was valued at.............................	300,000
Shingles, 104,104,500, at $4 per M.,..	416,418
Lath,..	123,000
Of the articles of headings, hoops, staves, etc., other than for salt barrels used here, there was shipped, in value,.. : ...	50,000
Of pine lumber proper, 457,396,225 feet, at $15 per M.,.................	6,860,943

Making the total product of lumber, of all descriptions, shipped in 1868 from Saginaw Valley...	$8,461,121

The manufacture of salt was commenced in the Valley in 1860, and the product has been as follows:

YEAR.	BARRELS.	YEAR.	BARRELS.
1860	4,000	1865	477,200
1861	125,000	1866	407 997
1862	243,000	1867	474,721
1863	466,356	1868	555,690
1864	529,073		

Total number of barrels,..	3,283,037
The product of 1868 amounting to	$1,111,380
By adding the value of lumber,.	8,461,121
It makes the total product of the Valley in the articles of lumber and salt alone,..	$9,572,501

In the whole State, including the above, there was manufactured, in 1868, 1, 600,000,000 feet, at $15 per M, amounting to:

Lumber,..	$24,000,000
Staves,......	1,648,040
Timber,...	1,000,000
Shingles,...	1,249,254
Lath,..	492,000
Hoops, heading, soft wood, staves, etc.,...........................	150,000
Total	$28,534,294

OF FISH.

	BARRELS.
During the year 1868 there were caught at Thunder Bay....................	7,000
At Harrisville, ...	5,500
At the Sauble, ...	30,000
In the Saginaw river and at the head of the Bay,...........................	4,000
Total,.	46,500
And valued at..	$325,500

Assuming this to be one-half the yield on the lake shores of the State, the value of the fish caught in the whole State in 1868 was $651,000.

PLASTER.

The extent and quality of the plaster beds at Alabaster, on the Saginaw Bay, are unsurpassed in this or any other State The exportation from there in 1868 was:

	TONS.
Of rock plaster,...	25,000
Of ground do. for land,...	2,000
Total	27,000

	BARRELS.
Of ground plaster,..	10,000
Of ground do., calcined,..	5,000
Total	15,000

I do not know the amount or value of the production of the Grand Rapids beds for this year, but the above exports from Alabaster brought in market $144,000.

From the foregoing statistics, which, when not taken from annual returns, are based upon careful estimates and comparisons, the gross value of the products of Northern Michigan, for the year 1868, inclusive of its agricultural, mechanical and several minor interests, was, from the forests, mines, quarries and fisheries alone, as follows :

Copper and Iron from Lake Superior,	$ 8,900,000
Lumber, timber, shingles, lath, staves, etc.,	28,534.294
Salt,	1,111.380
Fish,	651,000
Plaster,	144,000
Total,	$39,340,594

These figures are certainly not exaggerated, but much lower than other statements made by competent men, who have spent more time and labor in consulting the facts, but whose calculations, in some respects are believed to be too high.

A Northern Pacific Railroad on the Mackinaw route would reach the extensive quarries of marble which have been discovered (and supposed to be of the best quality) at the head of Menominee river, thus affording an outlet for the same.

It would also run through that splendid pine region lying between the Escanaba and Montreal rivers, a large portion of which is not reached either by the Escanaba, Menominee, Montreal or Ontonagon rivers, or their tributaries.

These forests, as well as those in the Lower Peninsula, away from the streams and on the line of the road, must furnish thousands of millions of lumber for transportation by rail.

The richest and most extensive deposits of iron, in what is called the Marquette District, are known to be on the line of this road, between the head waters of the Menominee and Lake Michigaumee. These vast and inexhaustible stores are sufficient to produce a million tons per annum for a century to come, and all of which must be brought to market by rail.

Every worker of iron knows that the charcoal pig of Lake Superior is unequalled in quality, and that its production heretofore has been entirely inadequate to the demand. This is in consequence of the spareness of hard wood, and the soft and poor quality growing in the vicinity of the mines, for charcoal, and for supplying the furnaces with fuel. On the recent visit of Mr. S. P. Ely to this city, (the Superintendent of the Marquette Railroad), knowing him to be a gentleman of much intelligence, and largely interested in the production and shipment of iron ore, I inquired of him how it was that they shipped the great bulk of iron in the ore, instead of first converting it into pig ; to save the profit and prevent the loss of freight to Cleveland on the dross ? His reply was as before stated, that it was for the want of hard wood, lime, &c., of which the lower Peninsula furnishes so vast an amount of the best quality. He added, "should a railroad be constructed across the Straits to the iron mines, furnaces and smelting works would be put in operation all along the line from Mackinaw to Saginaw, where the necessary materials for their successful operation are found without limitation as to quality or quantity."

This unquestionable result would not only furnish such a road with an unlimited amount of business, but would convert the forrests of hard wood into money instead of leaving them waste as at present; would clear the soil for the plow, rear villages, and people the line with thousands of industrious and thriving inhabitants. Not only so, but a Northern Pacific Railroad over the line suggested would soon be tapped by branches from the towns and mines on the copper range, and would thus secure the Spring, Fall and Winter travel and the freight of copper and supplies to and from the mines.

The forty million annual product of Northern Michigan would be increased to sixty millions, as most of the localities from which this product is realized would be reached by this road. If one-fifth of the passenger and freighting business was secured to the road, it would more than pay the entire cost of running from Superior to Saginaw River.

I was recently informed by an intelligent farmer, who cultivates a thousand acres about sixty miles west of St. Paul, in Minnesota, that the State produced twenty million bushels of wheat in 1868, and after much travel through that portion adapted to its growth, he gave it as his opinion, that not one acre in fifty had been cultivated. If, however, one-twentieth was used to produce the twenty million bushels, when all is sown with wheat the yield will be four hundred million of bushels

The Valleys of the Upper Missouri and Saskatchewan are as fine for the growth of wheat as Minnesota and embrace a territory five times as large. When they are peopled by agriculturist, as they soon will be, if railroad facilities are afforded, 2,000 million bushels of wheat can be produced, and all of which will seek an outlet by water, down the lakes, and by all the railroads that can be secured and reached.

This amount of wheat alone, as compared with the celebrated granaries of Egypt and the Black Sea, is as an ocean to a drop.

The Legislature of the State of Michigan, at its last session, passed an act ceding the Sault St. Mary Canal to the general Government, with a view of having it deepened to fourteen feet and made free to commerce. When this is done, and the Portage Canal, cutting off Keweenaw Point, is finished (thus materially shortening the distance, by water, from the Sault to the head of Lake Superior), and when the St. Paul and Superior, the Hudson, St. Croix and Superior and the Northern Pacific Railroads are completed to some point at the head of the lake, where a large city will be built, with its immense elevators and wharehouses to receive and discharge the freight, fifteen thousand vessels, instead of fifteen hundred, as at present, will annually pass through the Sault Canal.

The Mackinaw, and all other lines of Railroads from Chicago and other points connecting with the Northern Pacific, will require double tracks to do the business. This, too, without counting upon international or local business secured from the mineral regions west of the mountains.

If this line had been established, and, by reason of competition with other routes, had reduced the freight to the sea-board only five cents per bushel on wheat, the farmers of Minnesota would have saved thereby one million dollars on the crop of 1868.

The Trans-continental Railroad Convention recently held at Oswego, N. Y., appreciating the great necessity for the shortest and most direct Railroad connection with the Northern Pacific at the head of Lake Superior, after much able discussion and consideration, unamously adopted the following resolutions:

Resolved, by this Convention, That in forming a connection with the Northern Pacific Railroad at the head of Lake Superior, the shortest and most practical route should be adopted.

Resolved, That while in the opinion of this Convention, connections ought to and will be made *via* Chicago, the continuation of the N. P. R. R. to the Straits of Mackinaw, so as to connect with the contemplated road from Portland to the Detroit and St. Clair Rivers, ought also to be secured.

I am aware that the project of crossing the Sault River and passing through Canada to Montreal, and thence over to Vermont roads to Portland, has long been entertained by some of the officers of the N. P. R. R. Company, who are interested in said roads.

And I am also aware of the fact that this project becoming known, once defeated a subsidy to the N. P. Road by Congress.

This, while Canada remains a foreign country, ought not to be thought of. But that being the natural and by far the shortest route to the ocean, it can only in the nature of future events be delayed till Canada and the British possessions in North America become part of the United States. When that day comes, and come it soon must, the increased products of the North-West will create a necessity for that and all the other outlets to the East that can be secured, without injury to this or any other roads.

Finally, the only practical question to be considered is, *How shall this Convention aid in securing the speedy completion of the Northern Pacific Railroad by way of the Straits of Mackinaw?* I answer, by favoring in every possible, honorable way, Government aid to both such a Northern Pacific and a Southern Pacific Road. Such aid, either extended as security for the payment of the principal, or for the interest on the bonds of the roads, will secure their speedy completion. The Government can be amply secured against loss, by holding a mortgage on the lands and on all the property belonging to the corporations.

The liberal proposition will unite the strength of the North and South in Congress, and overcome any opposition the present Pacific Railroad might bring to bear against it. As a financial question in view of the National debt, if the roads are built, it is believed that the increase of population, of wealth, of commerce, and of taxable property, will make the nation richer instead of poorer, at the end of ten years, even if it should finally loose eighty or one hundred millions by becoming security.

This was the opinion expressed and maintained in a very able paper, prepared and read at the Oswego Convention, by Edwin F. Johnson, Esq., chief engineer of the Northern Pacific Railroad, and his views in this respect are concurred in by many prudent statesmen and thoughtful citizens. This eminent engineer also gives it as his opinion from practical knowledge, that there will be no serious difficulties met with in crossing the Straits of Mackinaw.

While living, Hon. Thaddeus Stevens was an ardent friend of the Northern Pacific Railroad by this route. He frequently told me when in conversation on the subject, that some day, not far in the future, one of the largest inland cities of the continent would be at the head of Lake Superior. In this opinion, I doubt not, he was correct.

At the conclusion of the reading of the foregoing paper, on motion of Mr. Hubbell, of Lake Superior, the thanks of the Convention were voted to Mr. Driggs, for his very able address.

Hon. D. H. Jerome, of Saginaw City, read the

REPORT OF THE COMMITTEE ON CREDENTIALS.

Showing the following named gentlemen to be entitled to seats as Delegates in this Convention : From

Ann Arbor—R. S. Smith.

Bay City—Jas Birney, H. M. Fitzhugh, C. C. Fitzhugh, D. H. Fitzhugh, Luther Westover, Wm. Westover, J. J. McCormick, J. McDermot, Geo. Campbell, J. J. Campbell.

Buena Vista—C. W. Kimball, Michael Leidlein, S. C. Munson.

Chesaning—F. P. Kenyon, R. H. Nason, R. W. Andrus, J. C. Goodale, R. P. Mason, Geo. W. Chapman.

Corunna—James Cummins, Hugh McCurdy, S. R. Kelsey, J. N. Ingersoll, E. F. Wade, E. C. Moore, D. Bush, O. S. Converse, J. B. Wheeler, Wm. Oaks, John L. Simonson.

Chicago, Ill.—J. H. Pearson

Detroit—Wm H. Craig, Luther Beecher, Wm. Phelps, James P. Mansfield, E. Reidy, John Burt, R. H. Anderson, H. H. Emmons, J. D. Standish, F. W. Swift, Wm. A. Moore, Geo. S. Frost, Morgan Johnson, A. E. Bissell, M. M. Fisher.

East Saginaw—Jas. L. Ketcham, John F. Driggs, Geo. W. Peck, J. Fisher, W. J Bartow, Joe A. Hollon, C. K. Robinson, Wm. L. Webber, D. W. C. Gage, J. K. Rose, L. S. Lenheim, J. F. Brown, A. B. Wood, C. H. Gage, M. B. Hess, T Edsall, David Rust, C. Ortman, M. Jeffers, E. T. Judd, J. J. Wheeler, T. E. Doughty, L. W. Tisdale.

Flint—A. Thayer, J. W. Begole, R. W. Jenny, A. L. Aldrich, F. H. Rankin, A. B. Witherbee.

Grand Rapids—Wm. A. Howard.

Houghton—J. A. Hubbell, Ransom Sheldon.

Holly—J. B. Simonson.

Jackson—Eugene Pringle, Horace S. Ismon.

Lapeer—E. J. White.

Lansing—J. W. Longyear, Cyrus Hewett, A. N. Hart, A. E. Cowles, Alfred Bixby, D. L. Case.

Marquette—Hiram A. Burt.

Midland—John Larkin, James W. Cochrane, John Haynes, C. E. Ball, James S. Eastman, George A. Janes.

Mason—O. M. Barnes.

Monroe—A. J. Sawyer, D. A. Noble, Edwin Willitts, T. R. Little, J. Wall, G. W. Strong, H. J. Redfield, C. Ives, J. R. Rauch, J. E. Ilginpitz, A. Darber, A. G. Bates, Charles Toll, E. G. Morton, T. Doyle, J. McLoure, M. D. Hamilton.

Northville—J. S. Lapham.

Oswego, N. Y.—A. S. Page, B. Doolittle, George Goble, R. Lippincott, C. Doolittle, Jno. A. Barry.

Owosso—B. O. Williams, D. Gould, A L. Williams.

Plymouth—C. H. Bennett.

Port Huron—O. D. Conger, J W. Sanborn, Edgar White, Cyrus Miles, John Miller, W. L. Bancroft, D. B. Harrington.

Portsmouth—Albert Miller.

Saginaw City—A. F. R. Braley, A. W. Wright, John Moore, D. H. Jerome, N. Barnard, W. S. Green, Daniel Hardin, C. T. Brenner, Thomas Merrill, Benton Hanchett, E. Briggs, James Haye, J. F. Adams, Ezra Rust, J. H. Sutherland.

Salem, State of Oregon—David Miller.

St. Clair—John E. Kilton, M. H. Miles, A. J. Chapman, Wm. Grace, Eugene Smith, B. W. Jenks.

St. Johns—Hon. Randolph Strickland.

Tuscola—J. H. Richardson, D. G. Slafter, W. H. Harrison, J. A. McPherson.

Toledo, Ohio.—A. E. McCumber, H. A. Boyd.

Vassar—B. W. Huston, Dr. Wm. Johnson, T. North, F. Bournes, Alexander Trotter, S. A. Lane.

Watrousville—H. P. Atwood.

Wenona—H. W. Sage, T. F. Sheppard, Jas. B. Ten Eyck, H. H. Wheeler, Frank Fitzhugh.

On motion, the report of the Committee was accepted and adopted.

Hon Wm. Phelps, of Detroit, presented, as the

REPORT OF THE COMMITTEE ON PERMANENT ORGANIZATION,

The names of the following persons as officers for the permanent organization of the Convention :

For President—Hon. JOHN MOORE, of Saginaw.

Vice Presidents
- JOHN McLAREN, of Monroe.
- JOSIAH W BEGOLE, of Flint.
- JOHN BURT, of Detroit.
- RANSOM SHELDON, of Houghton.
- HORACE S. ISMON, of Jackson.
- B. O. WILLIAMS, of Owosso.
- MARCUS H. MILES, of St. Clair.
- LUTHER WESTOVER, of Bay City.
- B. W. HUSTON, of Vassar.

Secretaries
- WILLIAM PHELPS, of Detroit.
- F. H. RANKIN, of Flint.
- MICHAEL JEFFERS, of East Saginaw.

The report of the Committee was adopted; and the gentlemen named took their places on the platform.

On being introduced to the Convention by Mr. Driggs, Hon. John Moore, in assuming the Chair, made the following remarks :

GENTLEMEN OF THE CONVENTION.—I am somewhat accustomed to the uncertainty that attends the rendition of a verdict by a petit jury. It has been said that before its rendition what such verdict will be is as uncertain as where lightning will strike. If I had received a slight shock of lightning, I should not have been more astonished than I am in being called upon to preside over the deliberations of this convention.

I appreciate the honor of being called upon to preside over a convention like this, of gentlemen assembled from all portions of our State and adjoining States, to deliberate upon a question of the importance of that submitted to the consideration of this convention. You have assembled irrespective of locality and irrespective of party predilections, to counsel together with regard to a great National enterprise.

The large attendance here to-day, and the interest already manifested in these proceedings, argue well for the success of the contemplated enterprise. The character of the gentlemen who have here assembled, show that the questions to be considered have engaged the attention of business men ; that they are questions, not of an hour or a day, but that they are the developements of a great necessity, growing out of the unexampled growth of the business interests of our State and Nation. The paper, or report, which has been read to the convention by the Hon. John F. Driggs, giving as it does in detail a full statement of the great interests to be developed and promoted by the construction of the Northern Pacific Railroad, and the great benefits that will result to this State and the Nation at large, by such a road, have brought to your mind clearly the magnitude of the undertaking and the necessity of this great National enterprise.

There is no necessity that I should trespass upon your time by any further reference to the subject that has brought you together. It is one I have no doubt that has received your consideration. It could not have been otherwise. The importance of the enterprise is well understood. Any assistance that I can give you in your deliberations, or that I can hereafter render to promote the building of the road through our State, will be a pleasure on my part. With this feeling I accept the position you have assigned me, and thank you for the honor of serving you upon this platform.

Hon. George W. Peck moved that a Committee of seven members be appointed by the Chair, to report Resolutions, and an Order of Business, for the consideration of the Convention; which motion prevailed.

The President appointed as such

COMMITTEE ON RESOLUTIONS, ETC.

Geo. W. Peck and John F. Driggs, of East Saginaw; H. M. Fitzhugh, of Bay City; W. H. Craig, of Detroit; Artemas Thayer, of Flint; H. A. Burt, of Marquette; and Eugene Pringle of Jackson.

The Convention then adjourned until seven oclock P. M.

EVENING SESSION.

The Convention re-assembled pursuant to adjournment, and was called to order by the President.

Hon. Geo. W. Peck, for the Committee on Resolutions and Order of Business, announced that the Committee would not be prepared to report before to-morrow morning.

At the request of a Delegate, the Call under which this Convention had assembled, was read by one of the Secretaries.

An interesting discussion of the objects of the Convention then took place, and was continued to a late hour. It was participated in by Hon. Wm. A. Howard, of Grand Rapids; H. H. Emmons, Esq., of Detroit; Hon. John F. Driggs, of East Saginaw; Hon. Randolph Strickland, of St. Johns; and John A. Barry, Esq., of Oswego, N. Y.

At the close of Mr. Barry's remarks, on motion, the Convention adjourned until 10 o'clock to-morrow morning.

SECOND DAY.

MORNING SESSION.

The Convention was called to order at 10 o'clock, A. M. on Wednesday, November 24th.

Mr. John Burt, of Detroit, being called upon, addressed the Convention in favor of the route proposed, representing to the Convention the great facilities and advantages of the extension through the Upper Peninsula of Michigan, from information of the nature of the territory, derived from his personal explorations of many years, as a surveyor.

THE PRESIDENT: There has just been placed in my hands a letter from Hon. Austin Blair, M. C., which the Secretary will read.

LETTER FROM EX-GOVERNOR BLAIR.

JACKSON, Nov. 23, 1869.

HON. JAS. L. KETCHAM, JOHN F. DRIGGS and other Committee, &c.

GENTLEMEN: I am wholly unable to attend the Convention at East Saginaw to-day, to which you were so kind as to invite me. My regret on this account is the greater that during the past summer I have had occasion to visit Puget Sound, and to become some acquainted with the needs and capabilities of that important region of our country.

The building of one railroad to the Pacific Ocean has served to prove how much we need two more. And especially to us of the northern portion of our country has it proved the necessity of the road to Puget Sound. To the great body of our people this is still to a great extent an unknown region, possessed of a cold and rigorous climate and valuable for little except lumber and timber, far away on the road to Alaska and eternal snow.

Nothing could be further from the truth. The climate of the country lying around this magnificent Sound is milder and more genial than that of our older States. The soil is rich and fertile, producing abundantly all the crops that belong to this zone. There are nearly fifteen hundred miles of coast all easily accessible to shipping, lying around this Sound and the bays that form a part of it.

Beyond all doubt here is to be the seat of a vast commerce and the homes of a numerous population. As a gateway to China and the Indies it is superior to the Bay of San Francisco.

There is no longer a doubt that the Northern route is more practicable at all seasons of the year than the Central. Besides it is *our route* above all others and cannot fail to commend itself to the good judgment of our people.

I should be glad to have been with you at this important convention, and to have joined in its discussions, but since that may not be, I shall hope still to aid you efficiently in other fields of your enterprise.

I sympathize entirely with your objects and will promote them in all proper ways.

Very Respectfully, Your Obedient Servant,

AUSTIN BLAIR.

Mr. Peck : Before proceeding to discharge my duty as Chairman of the Committee on Resolutions, permit me to read to the Convention a letter from Mr. Johnson, the Engineer of the Northern Pacific Railroad.

LETTER FROM E. F. JOHNSON, C. E.

Middleton, Ct., Nov. 15th, 1869.

To Hon. Jas. L. Ketcham, John F. Driggs, and others, Committee, etc., East Saginaw, Michigan.

Gentlemen : It will not be in my power to comply with your invitation to be present at the convention at your place on the 23d inst., or to express in writing, at any length, my views upon the interesting topics to be discussed by the convention. These, so far as the Northern Pacific road is concerned, were very fully stated to the convention lately held at Oswego, and will appear in their proceedings. For my general views as to the need of additional railway lines east of the Mississippi, and reasons therefor, I refer to my published report of last year, made to the Ontario Shore Railroad Company.

The Northern Pacific road, when built, is to have its eastern terminus, as provided in its charter, at some point on Lake Superior, within the States of Wisconsin or Minnesota. This point has not yet been determined. The Northern Pacific Company, so far as I know, do not contemplate asking Congress for any extension of their line towards the east beyond their present chartered limits. But if the country demands such extension, they will not, I presume, oppose it, but will carry out, in good faith, whatever is required of them by the Government.

Upon the subject of a line of railway from near the western extremity of Lake Superior to a connection with lines leading to Port Huron or Detroit, by the Straits of Mackinaw, I can say that, from my knowledge of the country south of Lake Superior, derived from observation and otherwise, the ground is in general favorable, and free from obstructions of a serious character, and will nowhere probably require a gradient exceeding 40 feet to the mile.

Passing from this region to Michigan proper, the principal impediment is the Straits of Mackinaw, which is three and one-half miles from Point La Barbe, on one side, to Point McGalpin upon the other, with an average depth of water from 65 to 70 feet, and a maximum depth of 216 feet, sufficient to deter from any attempt at bridging.

The passage of this strait by railway trains can, however, be very economically and expeditiously made, and, I think, at all seasons, by means of boats constructed for the purpose.

As to Michigan proper, or Lower Michigan, the face of the country is known to be very favorable for the construction of a road, with easy gradients. It is nowhere marked by any very strong features of a character to require extraordinary expense in the building of a road.

So far, therefore, as regards the line as a whole, the important question is whether the business and resources of the country through which it will pass are such as to justify its construction.

My own opinion is, that viewed as a local road only, it will eventually be well sustained. That portion of it lying west of Lake Michigan will have large mineral resources. The ores of iron now so extensively mined near Lake Superior are situated at Neguanee and vicinity, near the line of the railway to Marquette, on Lake Superior, on one side, and to Escanaba, on the little Bay de Noquet, on Lake Michigan, on the other.

From these mines are now shipped to southern and eastern markets over 300,000 tons of iron ore annually. To the south and west of this locality, near the divide of the Lake Superior and Mississippi waters, and extending west as far as the western extremity of the lake, there are other deposits of iron ore equally rich and extensive.

These latter, together with the copper, which is scattered throughout the same region will come within the influence of the proposed road and be developed by it. There are also in the same region large and valuable tracts of pine lands, the lumber of which will find its way to market over the road. The soil of this region in Wisconsin and especially in Upper Michigan, is in general, sandy and light, but there are considerable portions well adapted to cultivation which will be fully improved to supply the wants of the mining and lumbering population that will gather within its limits.

The line from Mackinaw, south, passes centrally through lower Michigan in a position favorable for commanding the business of that portion of the State. This portion is being rapidly settled. In addition to the farm products of the soil, it has extensive groves of pine and other timber and embraces within its limits a large part of the coal basin and the Salt Springs of Central Michigan.

The above remarks apply mainly to the local business of the proposed road. If an enterprise of this character will stand this test, its success may be deemed certain, for all lines of railway, wherever situated, invariably attract largely to their support the business of the more remote sections of the country.

Passing, as the proposed line does for much of its extent, through an undeveloped region, it will require the aid which the Government has, in similar cases, bestowed—a grant of the Government lands in alternate sections within a limited distance on either side of it. The aid thus given, when judiciously conferred upon lines that are really meritorious, enriches both the Government and the country. This is shown by the stimulus it has imparted to the building of railways in the newer sections of the country, and the rapid advance in those sections in population and in taxable wealth.

With best wishes that the action of your convention may result beneficially to Michigan and the country at large,

I am, gentlemen, very respectfully yours,
EDWIN F. JOHNSON,
Civil Engineer.

MR. RUST: I would remark to the Convention that Mr. Johnson's letter was written some time ago, and the past season shows an aggregate shipment of over 700,000 tons of iron ore.

MR. PECK: Mr. President—As Chairman of the Committee on Resolutions, I beg leave to report that the Committee deem it inexpedient to report any Rules, Regulations, or Order of Business.

They instruct me to submit Resolutions, which I will now proceed to read:

REPORT OF COMMITTEE ON RESOLUTIONS.

Resolved, That Railroads through the Northern Peninsula of the State of Michigan to the Straits of Mackinaw, and thence by direct connection with the East and North, are demanded by the interest, not only of Michigan, but of the whole country, and that such roads developing mining. lumbering, manufacturing, commercial, and agricultural interests of the first importance, will necessarily have the effect to transmute five hundred miles of wilderness into one of the most productive and richest sections of the Union.

Resolved, That such roads are necessary in justice to Michigan as a bond of Union between its two Peninsulas, and to continue by a practical and the shortest route towards the Atlantic, that future great

continental highway, of which the Northern Pacific Road will form a
part, and that in the judgment of this Convention it is the imparative
duty of Congress to extend the land grants now held by the Jackson,
Lansing & Saginaw, and the Grand Rapids and Indiana Railroad Companies, to the Straits of Mackinaw, relieving these Companies of the
requirement to terminate upon Little Traverse Bay, and also to make
such liberal grants of land, money or credit, as shall secure the speedy
construction of the road from the present Eastern terminus of the
Northern Pacific Road to the Straits of Mackinaw

Resolved, That the Convention deems it the true policy of the country to extend to such projects, as those of Railroads from Mackinaw to
Puget Sound, and upon the line of the proposed Southern Pacific Road,
such aid as will secure their speedy construction, and that we may cite
the prosperity of such States and Districts as have been liberal in aid-
ing great public works, as a perpetual argument to show the safety
and wisdom of such a policy.   •

Resolved, That there be appointed by this Convention a committee of
seven persons whose duty it shall be, by petitions to Congress, by explorations and by such continued public agitation of the subject, as
may be necessary, to use all ligitimate efforts to secure the necessary
legislation and investments of capital, and that it shall be the duty of
such committee to appeal to the people and corporations more immediately interested for the means to defray the expense of such efforts.

Resolved, That while the said roads of Michigan and the Northwest,
as pioneers in the developement of our own and neighboring State, (as
far as their system is completed) are entitled to our highest consideration, and demand the warmest encouragement and sopport, from this
Convention, and the people we represent ; we do more especially and
earnestly call upon Congress, to extend Government aid, in such effi-
cient form as it may deem best, to secure the construction of the
Northern Pacific Railroad to the Straits of Mackinaw, as the most important of all our Railroad interests.

Resolved, That the Committee appointed by this Convention, under
the foregoing resolutions, be and they are hereby instructed, to insti-
tute inquiry into the condition, prospects, and purposes of the Northern Pacific Railroad Company, as at present organized, and if it shall
satisfactorily appear. that the grant made to that Company, for the
construction of its road, is likely to lapse or become forfeited ; or such
construction to be unreasonably delayed,—they are hereby instructed
to bring the subject before Congress, and to urge its immediate action
to compel or secure, the immediate commencement of the work in good
faith ; and its completion at the earliest practicable period.

Resolved, That the Secretaries of this Convention furnish to the
President of the United States, and to the members of his Cabinet, cer-
tified copies of these resolutions, and printed copies of the proceedings
of this Convention ; and when Congress meets, furnish the President
of the Senate, the Speaker of the House of Representatives, the Chair-
men of the several Rail Road Committees; and of the Committees of
Ways and Means, and Finance, respectively, with like copies of these
resolutions and proceedings.

The report of the Committee on Resolutions was accepted, and
a motion made and carried, that the Convention proceed to consider the resolutions separately and *seriatim*.

The first resolution being then under consideration, Mr. Luther
Beecher, of Detroit, addressed the Convention at some length, and
offered the following preamble and resolutions :

MR. BEECHER'S RESOLUTIONS.

WHEREAS, Large amounts of Government Land, in the States of Michigan and Wisconsin have for many years been in market, unsold and unpopulated to the great damage and detriment of large portions of both States; and

WHEREAS, Said Lands cannot be sold or occupied, even at the lowest graduation price of one shilling per acre, until water or Railway transit lines shall be constructed so as to pass through or near them; and

WHEREAS, These results cannot be otherwise so song as *this* state of things remains unchanged, by coming possibility prove advantageous to the nation; and

WHEREAS, The early extension of the Great Northern Pacific Rail road from the head of Lake Superior, Eastward, through the States of Wisconsin and Michigan is of vastly more importance to both States and of the whole Nation than any possible values of said lands; Therefore it is

Resolved, That it is for the National interest to surrender all of the unsold lands in each of said States to their respective Governors *in trust* the whole proceeds thereof to be expended in construction of such Trunk lines of Transit and such branches as shall best accomplish the ten fold purpose of selling and populating their land and aid in *construction of Railway and Water Transit lines*, demanded by the vast growth of the great NorthWestern States.

Resolved, That said lands ought to be appraised and graded in value and *all* of them subject to sale for Cash or "Land Scrip", Freight, Transit, Bonds, Stock, or other evidences of value used in construction of said Trunk lines or Branches, and that the "Legislation" necessary for this purpose should be *prompt and of the most liberal character*.

Resolved, That as an offset for such surrender, of what is of no practical value to the General Government, but may be made of much value to the said States and of the Nation—in the manner proposed.—Said States can well afford to surrender, and forever relinquish, any and all unsettled war claims for bounties or other aid furnished by counties, town, cities or individuals—supposed to amount to about 3 or $4,000,000 *in each State*, while the lands, say 9,000,000 of acres in Wisconsin and 10,000,000 of acres in Michigan would only amount to about $3,000,000 at graduation value.

On motion, the preamble and resolutions of Mr. Beecher were referred to the Committee on Resolutions.

Hon. Eugene Pringle, of Jackson, was called upon, and discussed at length the resolution under consideration and the objects of the Convention.

At the close of Mr. Pringle's speech, the Convention adjourned until two o'clock in the afternoon.

AFTERNOON SESSION.

At two o'clock P. M., pursuant to adjournment, the Convention was called to order by the President.

Hon. O. M. Barnes, of Mason, and Dr. H. C. Potter, of East Saginaw, were severally called for, and addressed the Convention,

illustrating their remarks by reference to a large map, produced
by Mr. Barnes, showing the location, etc., of the land grants made
to the Michigan Railroads.

The question was then taken upon the first resolution of the
Committee, and the same was adopted.

The second resolution being again read, Mr. J. A. Hubbell, of
Houghton, made a speech in its favor, after which the resolution
was adopted.

The third resolution was then read, and was supported in a
speech of some length by Hon. George W. Peck. The resolution
was then adopted.

The fourth resolution was then adopted.

On the fifth resolution being read, Mr. Emmons moved to amend
the resolution by striking out the words " to secure the construc-
" tion of the Northern Pacific Railroad to the Straits of Macki-
" naw," and insert, in lieu thereof, the words " to extend the route
" of the Northern Pacific Railroad to the Straits of Mackinaw," and
advocated his proposed amendment in remarks at some extent.

The amendment was opposed by Messrs. Peck, Driggs and Pringle, and was withdrawn by the mover.

Mr. Emmons asked the indulgence of the Convention while he
offered a personal explanation ; and proceeded to make some remarks in reference to his address to the Convention on the previous
evening, elucidating more clearly the position he occupied.

The fifth resolution was then adopted.

The sixth and seventh resolutions were severally adopted.

The President : Gentlemen of the Convention, by the resolutions you have passed, you have provided for the appointment of a
Committee of Seven. The resolution does not specify how that
Committee shall be appointed. I suppose, under ordinary Parlia-
mentary rules, the Chair should appoint that Committee, but I
decline to exercise that power. I think the Convention will see
the impropriety of the exercise of that power by myself.

All local jealousies and feeling and controversy have been kept
out of this Convention ; and there are points along the line of this
road that have their own local interests, which it is proper for
them to look after. I reside at one of those points ; and it might

be claimed that I exercised the power which I would thus exercise to favor the ends of my own particular locality. I therefore insist that the Convention adopt some means by which that Committee shall be appointed.

Mr. Emmons moved that it be 'referred to the Committee on resolutions.

Mr. Peck moved as a substitute, that the Chair appoint a [Committee of Five, to recommend the names of persons to the Convention, for appointment as a Committee required under the resolution.

The substitute was adopted, and the Chair appointed as such Committee: C. K. Robinson, of East Saginaw; C. C. Fitzhugh, of Bay City; H. A. Rust, of Marquette; W. H. Craig, of Detroit and W. S. Green, of Saginaw.

While awaiting the report of this Committee, the following additional letters on the objects of the meeting, were read to the Convention:

LETTER FROM ALFRED MEAD.

ONTONAGON, MICH., Nov. 13, 1869.

HON. JOHN F. DRIGGS,

DEAR SIR:

Your circular letter calling a Railroad Convention at Saginaw, on the 23d inst., has just reached me, and I at once send you a few lines to wish you and your friends God speed. It will be almost impossible for any one to attend from our county, (for you know we have no means of getting out and in the country at this time of the year), much as I wish that some of us would, had it been earlier or later, I would cheerfully have come myself, for you know I feel that a Railroad connecting us with the outer world is our only hope of relief from our present depressed condition.

But as we cannot attend, we shall feel confident that you, dear sir, will represent us and our views and watch our interests. Say to the gentlemen of that Convention that the people of Ontonagon will do all in their power to aid in the object of the Convention. We want a Railroad and will extend our aid to the first parties that approach us with any reasonable plan that will guarantee us the object, whether from the East, Michigan or Chicago. Of our situation and resources I need say but little, with them you are acquainted, also the attempts of Railroad Cos. to connect heretofore with us, but allow me to call your attention to one or two points. You are aware that the grant to the Ontonagon & Marquette Railroad Co. has been declared forfeited by the Legislature, this grant

is now open for other parties to take hold of, it is a grant from
the U. S. of ten Sections per mile, but twenty miles of that road
has been built, and we venture to say, whoever will fill the gap
between here and the road at these Iron Mines will reap large re-
wards. By the act of the Legislature any corporation upon whom
this grant is conferred, are required to build fifteen miles of this
end of the road, commencing at Ontonagon Village. To aid in
the construction of the fifteen miles, this county as particularly interested, and we will lend our aid. To any corporation that will
do it we will confer a State Swamp Land grant of two Sections
per mile, the scrip is worth now, I believe, about 80 or 85 cents
on the dollar, and is easily convertible into cash. From the best
information we can obtain, the two Sections of Scrip will build
the Road bed ready for the Iron, in fact, parties here (of no experience in road building) have offered to take the first ten miles,
and get it ready for the iron, for the two Sections of Swamp Land.

As to the location of Ontonagon I am not the only one that
thinks that it would be a favorable point for the commencement of
the Northern Pacific. But I claim that road can have no *terminus*
till it is connected with the rail road system of Michigan,
and its most natural route, as through the Upper Peninsula,
whether it will make connections at the Sault St. Marie or Mackinaw, it is for the people of Michigan to decide. The indications
are that Old and New England Capital will make a desperate
effort to cross at the Sault St. Marie, and the route has undoubt-
edly great advantages, but we shall see to it that it crosses our
own territory. Hoping that the Convention may be well attended
and its deliberations result in an effort to give us road out of the
country. I am Sir, Yours very respectfully,

                                              ALFRED MEAD.

LETTER FROM HIRAM WALKER.

To JAMES L. KETCHAM, Mayor of East Saginaw, and others.

MESSRS : I am in the receipt of your circular inviting the friends
of the Northern Pacific Railroad, and its connections now made
and to be made to form the shortest and most feasible route
from Puget Sound, on the Pacific, to Portland, in Maine, on the
Atlantic, to attend a Railroad Convention in your city on the 23d
inst., which I am unable to attend.

No one at all informed on the " advance of Empire West" doubts
the importance of these connecting lines of railroads, connecting
the Atlantic and Pacific States, and whoever lives twenty years
will see all these lines in operation. Who can tell the vast commercial interests that will flow through these channels ? The Erie
canal made the city of New York the metropolis of America, and
these Pacific Railroads will make these United States the business
center of the world. This is no myth.

The first railroad in the United States, of any note, was the Albany and Schenectady, which was completed in August, 1832; and the first line of telegraph in May, 1840, between Baltimore and Washington. And now what a network of railroads and telegraph lines do these States present. Computation would almost fail to show their cost of construction, much less to show the advance in value of real estate caused by their construction. San Francisco is nearer Boston, in point of time, than was the Valley of the Hudson one hundred years ago. If so much has been done in thirty-seven years, when large sums have been lost in experimenting, what grand results may be looked for in 1900.

Xerxes threw golden fetters into the sea to restrain the billows, in his anguish of defeat; but American skill and genius, with indomitable perseverance, has tunneled mountains, spanned mighty rivers, and strode triumphantly over the snow-clad Alps of America with the iron horse, which needed no rest from Plymouth Rock to the "Golden Gate." If such things are done in the "dry tree," what may we expect from the "green tree?"

"The wealth of Indies" will flow through these channels, aside from pecuniary gain. They will prove powerful agents of civilization by extending a knowledge of our free institutions. It will aid the missionary in the cause of evangelizing the world, and promote the cause of peace among the nations of the earth. Europe can reach China and Japan quicker and cheaper than by any other route, These roads will cement the interests of the different sections of this Union into one mighty Empire, and give us prestige among the nations of the earth; so that rock-bound New England, with its busy wheels and spindles, the rich alluvial soil of the Valley of the Mississippi, and the golden Pacific slope, may have a common interest in keeping this Government intact through ages to come.

Another consideration which should exert a powerful influence in favor of constructing this "Trans-Continental Railroad" is the fact that the Valley of the Mississippi, which is to be the great granary of the world, needs a cheaper and more ample outlet to the sea-board for her surplus products, and these products are increasing faster than the avenues of transportation are. So long as the producers can get a remunerative price for their products, so long they will patronize the mechanical interests of New England; but when they are compelled to retain them, for want of a ready outlet of their surplus products, at a fair home valuation, there will be a hegira of the wheels and spindles to the Mississippi Valley, which, like the "ten lost tribes," will never return.

There are two routes proposed by which to reach Lake Ontario from Portland. One is to strike Lake Champlain through Northern New Hampshire and Vermont, near Rouse's Point; thence by Ogdensburg to Oswego or Syracuse, N. Y. Another is to cross Connecticut river near Woodstock, Vt., thence to Rutland, Vt., and Whitehall, N. Y., at the head of Lake Champlain, thence to

Saratoga, to escape the spurs of the Adirondacks, thence westerly, north of the Central, to the Valley of Salmon river, thence to Oswego. The remainder of the route to St. Paul was too well delineated at the late Convention at Oswego to need repeating here.

Wishing you harmony and important action in your Convention about to meet, and that agitation will not cease until permanent measures are adopted for the construction of this important line of intercommunication,

I remain, gentleman,
Very respectfully yours,
HIRAM WALKER.

P. S. Please send me an account of your Convention.

MEXICO, N. Y., Nov. 16, 1869.

LETTER FROM WM. A. THOMPSON.

QUEENS HOTEL, TORONTO, Nov. 22, 1869.

JOHN F. DRIGGS, Esq.,
East Saginaw.

MY DEAR SIR :—I should certainly have responded to the invitation, and attended your Convention, but that I am tied down here by duties of the greatest importance, and which will hold me here for a fortnight When we get the Niagara, Detroit & St. Clair River Railway fairly floated, you will find me ready to respond to you, every effort of making a Great Through Line to the Northern Pacific *via* Saginaw.

I am, my dear sir, yours very truly,
WM. A. THOMSON.

You notice we are changing the name of our Railway.

MR. ROBINSON, from the Committee on nominations, reported the names of the following gentlemen, to compose the Committee of Seven, to be appointed under the provisions of the fourth resolution, viz :

STANDING COMMITTEE OF SEVEN.

JOHN F. DRIGGS, of East Saginaw.
JOHN RUST, of Detroit.
ARTEMAS THAYER, of Flint.
H. M. FITZHUGH, of Bay City.
JOHN MOORE, of Saginaw City.
J. A. HUBBELL, of Houghton.
S. P. ELY, of Marquette.

On motion, the report was accepted, and the nominations of the Committee, as above, ratified.

Mr. Driggs regreted to be obliged positively to decline acting as Chairman of the Committee ; and Mr. Moore also asked to be excused from serving as a member; but the Convention refused to make any change in the constitution of the Committee as reported.

On motion, the members of the Committee were authorized to appoint substitutes, in case any of them should be unable to attend to the business assigned them.

On motion of Hon. George W. Peck, the Secretaries were instructed to have not less than one thousand copies of the proceedings of the Convention printed in pamphlet form, for distribution.

The thanks of the Convention were voted to the President, Vice-Presidents and Secretaries, for the faithful performance of their duties ; to the Reporters of the Press, for their full and impartial reports of the proceedings ; to Capt. Kirby and Messrs. E. G. Godard and W. H. Herbert for furnishing the large and complete map used by the Convention ; and to Mr. W. J. Bartow, for the use of Irving Hall.

The President, in a few remarks, thanked the Convention for the very harmonious manner in which they had conducted their business, and wished them success in the great undertaking they had inaugurated.

On motion, the Convention adjourned *sine die*.

JOHN MOORE, *President.*

JOHN McLAREN,
JOSIAH W. BEGOLE,
JOHN BURT,
RANSOM SHELDON,
HORACE S. ISMON,   } *Vice Presidents.*
B. O. WILLIAMS,
MARCUS H. MILES,
LUTHER WESTOVER,
B. W. HUSTON,

WILLIAM PHELPS,
F. H. RANKIN,   } *Secretaries.*
MICHAEL JEFFERS,

APPENDIX.

Actual Products of Iron Ore and Pig Metal in the Marquette District.

From the Saginaw Daily Enterprise, of December 1st, 1869.

EAST SAGINAW, Nov. 30, 1869.

To THE EDITOR OF THE ENTERPRISE.

SIR :—I send you for publication a letter just received from Hiram A. Burt, Esq., Collector of Customs, at Marquette, Lake Superior. It will be seen that his statement of the yield of iron in the Lake Superior region during the present year, 1869, makes the same nearly one hundred thousand tons more than given in your table of figures in the paper read to the Convention. It was my purpose in the paper referred to (and which was prepared without much time) to be as accurate as possible, and where my figures were not made up from actual returns, to place them below rather than above what subsequent facts might prove to be correct. Before placing the product of iron at 600,000 tons. I inquired of Mr. S. P. Ely, of Marquette, as to the amount for 1869, and he informed me that while he did not yet know the exact amount, I would certainly be safe in placing it at 600,000 tons.

It now appears from Mr. Burt's statement, which is doubtless correct, that the yield is 696,030 tons, valued at $5,185,398, being in excess over the value as fixed by my figures, $935,398. I hardly think it possible that my calculations as to lumber and other products, will be found so much a varience with the facts, as they are based upon returns of former years. But I am confident, if not strictly correct, they will prove to be below instead of above the mark. The larger yield of iron, it will be seen, makes the product of Northern Michigan over $40,000,000.

J. F. DRIGGS.

HON. JOHN F. DRIGGS, East Saginaw.

DEAR SIR:—I notice, on reading the published report of your able paper, read before the late Railroad Convention in your city, that you so much under-estimate the present year's production of iron ore and pig metal in the Marquette Iron District, that I desire to give you the actual figures up to Nov. 15th.

The actual product of Iron Ore is .... 629 489 gross tons.
Estimated product balance of year .... 30 000   "

    Total product Ore ....657 487 gross tons.
Pig Metal to Nov. 15th, ... 35 543 gross tons.
Estimated product balance of year .... 3 000   "   38 543   "

    Total of Ore and Pig Metal....................................696 030   "
Value... $ 5 185 898
Increased production over 1869................................... 149 971
    "   value   "   .... $ 1 182 985

With regard to future production, I know of blast furnaces enough now building to increase the demand for ore next year fully 150,000 tons, thus realizing, in 1870, your prophecy as to what must take place upon the construction of the Northern Pacific Railroad; 800,000 tons in 1870, and 1,000,000 in 1872, are my prediction of the requirement from the Lake Superior Iron Mines in those years. What would be the result of the construction of the Northern Pacific Railroad is beyond calculation.

Yours, Respectfully,
HIRAM A. BURT.

www.ingramcontent.com/pod-product-compliance
Lightning Source LLC
Chambersburg PA
CBHW021642270326
41931CB00008B/1120